DISTRACTIONS, DISTORTIONS, DECEPTIONS, AND OUTRIGHT LIES

DIVERSIONS THAT KEEP THE SOUTH RED, POOR PEOPLE POOR, AND PLUTOCRATS AND OLIGARCHS IN POWER

VAL ATKINSON

Order this book online at www.trafford.com
or email orders@trafford.com

Most Trafford titles are also available at major online book retailers.

Print information available on the last page.

ISBN: 978-1-4907-8682-7 (sc)
ISBN: 978-1-4907-8684-1 (hc)
ISBN: 978-1-4907-8683-4 (e)

Library of Congress Control Number: 2018900075

Trafford rev. 02/01/2018

Trafford
PUBLISHING® www.trafford.com
North America & international
toll-free: 1 888 232 4444 (USA & Canada)
fax: 812 355 4082

Contents

How conservatives use God, guns, gays, gestation (abortion), genealogy (race, ethnicity, and gender), and "gubment" (rights and taxes) to deceive voters into voting against their economic self-interest.

For more than a half century since the passage of the 1965 Voting Rights Act, conservatives have used these diversions to keep voters (mainly white working-class voters) staunchly affixed to the conservative philosophy.

But few of the Right's strategies would work without the witting and unwitting cooperation of some of our well-meaning liberal and progressive Democrats and their unwavering commitment to bipartisanship through compromise. Compromise can be useful, and even necessary, if we are to have a functioning democracy, but lest we forget *unilateral*, compromise is not just an oxymoron, but it can also be a synonym for capitulation.

Dedication

To my late parents, Earl and Cora Atkinson, and my three grandsons, Victor Lorenzo Atkinson of Portsmouth, Virginia, and Graham Batiste St. Cyr and Ellis Batiste St. Cyr of Columbia, Maryland.

If you can dream it, YOU CAN DO IT.

—**Walt Disney**

Foreword

Johnson Lassiter Atkinson
BA Political Science, BS Economics—UNC-C
JD—Duke University

In today's world of the twenty-four-hour news cycle and Instagram attention spans, it is more important than ever to learn to see through the fog of distractions and to bring the critical issues of our time into clearer focus. Whether it's career politicians trying to get a quick vote, cable news outlets chasing ratings, or the establishment making sure that the disfavored and disenfranchised stay in their places, there's no shortage of people and things willing to feed us an endless stream of distractions. Sometimes we're fed these distractions to prevent us from focusing on the pressing issues, and sometimes our inability to concentrate on the real problems is merely an unfortunate by-product of an individual or entity's self-interested pursuits. In either event, our ability to separate the wheat from the chaff has never been more critical to our progress. *Distractions* is about identifying and sifting through those talking points and hot topics that so often occupy our collective consciousness at the expense of the things that matter most. And it's about the strategies used to sell distractions.

Distractions takes us on a two-hundred-year journey through the evolution of conservative messaging to show that poor people have been led astray from the very beginning. It shows how leaders of the right wing have been able to consistently prevail on the economic and political issues they value most by creating distractions to assemble a coalition of the misinformed. *Distractions* also shows how the left wing has consistently lost ground in the ultimate battle for justice and socioeconomic equality because we have become so fixated on the distractions of the day that we can't see the proverbial *forest for the trees*.

Distractions pinpoints the survival and proliferation of unbridled exploitative[1] capitalism as the highest goal of the persons and entities who control the conservative wing of our political system. The book goes on to show how, through a barrage of buzzwords and hot topics, the controlling factions of the right wing have co-opted a variety of groups with disparate priorities to unite behind this conservative banner and ultimately (if not unintentionally) advance its prime motive.[2] As a result, many individuals who are directly and negatively influenced by the sort of ruthless capitalism advanced by the leaders of the Right will unwittingly protect the very systems and structures that oppress them.

Ingeniously, the buzzwords used to draw support for the conservative cause also serve a secondary purpose: distracting us—those disadvantaged and disenfranchised by the particular brand of capitalism propounded by the Right—from challenging the true source of our disempowerment. Unable to see the true heart of the issues, we rail against each perceived slight and small injustice. We focus all too often on the fluff, rarely targeting the core of the conservative agenda. As a result, while we might sometimes win victories on the battleground issues of the day, we are constantly losing the war against social, political, and economic oppression. As *Distractions* makes clear, we will never make real progress toward that democratic ideal of true justice and equality for all until we are able to focus our attention on the fundamental challenges we must overcome.

Nowhere are the dangers of distractions more pronounced than in the form of our sitting president, Donald J. Trump. In fact, one could say that Mr. Trump has crafted his entire public and political image from distractions. Much like his counterparts in the GOP (Grand Old Party) establishment, Mr. Trump seems to have (knowingly or unknowingly) harnessed and manipulated our addiction to sound bites and hot takes

---

1   Also used to describe predatory capitalism.

2   Right-wing agenda.

to achieve his goals. Employing a strategy never before seen in electoral politics, Mr. Trump repeatedly creates firestorms of controversy as a means of obfuscating the critical issues and draining our collective reserves of outrage. With every new inappropriate comment or political miscue, we grow more focused on what Mr. Trump says and how he says it rather than what he's doing and how his decisions affect the least powerful among us. And as long as we continue to allow ourselves to be blinded by the issue de jour, the fundamental unfairness of our society will never be fixed. The themes and thoughts of *Distractions* can help us focus more clearly on these critical and fundamental issues to the exclusion of the ceaseless bombardment of distractions.

Although Mr. Trump's particular method of utilizing distractions to enhance his political candidacy was somewhat unprecedented, the use of distractions by the Right to advance their central aims is nothing new. As *Distractions* adeptly shows, they've been doing it for years. Going all the way back to the Civil War, *Distractions* demonstrates how the Confederacy used distractions of racial identity and bigotry to inveigle legions of poor, disadvantaged whites to fight and die for a system that provided enormous financial benefits to their slave-owning counterparts. This theme of using race-identity politics to co-opt poor whites into voting and acting against their own economic self-interest was replicated in the 1960s, 1970s, and 1980s with the Southern strategy and continues to be employed today but more subtly. Convincing poor whites that ethnic minorities are more to blame for their discontent than the political, economic, and social systems that keep the rich wealthy and the poor disempowered was key to the success of the Nixon- and Reagan-era GOP and continues to be a subliminal undertone of conservative messaging today.

Hopefully, through the wisdom gleaned from these pages, each of us will be able to better prepare ourselves for this particular brand of political warfare and that we may one day have hope to meaningfully transform our society into the fair, just, and equitable democracy we all believe it can be. Hopefully, we can remember that we are not just fighting individual battles against ignorant or insensitive comments and one-off injustices but instead are also constantly engaged in a war for the future of our society. But until we are able to remain fixated on our true goals and able to brush aside the distractions of the day, meaningful progress will remain elusive.

Preface

This dynamic, which legal scholar Reva Siegel has dubbed "preservation through transformation," is the process through which white privilege is maintained, though the rules and rhetoric change. This process, though difficult to recognize at any given moment, is easier to see in retrospect. Since the nation's founding, African Americans repeatedly have been controlled through institutions, such as slavery and Jim Crow, which appear to die but then are reborn in new form, tailored to the needs and constraints of the time. As described in the pages that follow, there is a certain pattern to this cycle. Following the collapse of each system of control, there has been a period of confusiontransition—in which those who are most committed to — racial hierarchy search for a new means to achieve their goals within the rules of the game as currently defined. It is during this period of uncertainty that the backlash intensifies and a new form of racialized social control begins to take hold. The adoption of the new system of control is never inevitable, but to date, it has never been avoided. The most ardent proponents of racial hierarchy have consistently succeeded in implementing new racial caste systems by triggering a collapse of resistance across the political spectrum. *This fear has been achieved largely by appealing to the racism and vulnerability of lower class whites, a group of*

people who are understandably eager to ensure that they never find themselves
trapped at the bottom of the American hierarchy.[3]

—Michelle Alexander
The New Jim Crow

If you are a breathing, sane American (especially if you're a Democrat), you've gotta be asking yourself, "How do Republicans keep getting away with convincing poor white voters to vote against their economic self-interest?" The answer may be found in the Democrats' positions on campaign management. Democrats seem to have been convinced that they could win elections against Republicans by simply outvoting them with greater VR (voter registration) and GOTV[4] (get out the vote) efforts. Democrats also seem to think that all voters are interested in those issues that have direct impact on their daily lives like health care, jobs, education, housing, and nondiscrimination through fairness and equal opportunities. It saddens me to say that that's what Americans _should_ be interested in and motivated by, but that's not the case today, and Republicans have figured it out; Democrats, not so much. They're still working on it.

To properly unpack this assertion, we'll have to go back to the real beginning of the black vote in America—1966. Since the passage of the 1965 Voting Rights Act, Republicans have been exploring methods and means to discount and control the black vote. In 1968, Richard Nixon embarked on the "Southern strategy."[5] In 1972, he used "law and order"[6]

---

3   Michelle Alexander's take on the institution of racism in America, its origins, pillars, and proponents.

4   Getting out the vote is a very important strategy for the Democratic Party. Since the implementation of the 1965 Voting Rights Act, Democrats have concentrated on getting out the vote of newly registered African American voters.

5   The Southern strategy was invented by Harry Dent Sr. The primary purpose of the strategy is to maximize the number of Southern whites who vote for the Republican ticket. This was, and is, accomplished by denigrating black voters and scaring white voters.

6   Law and order was a dog whistle used by the Republicans to connote harsh treatment of blacks by law enforcement officials.

and "the war on ~~black folk~~ drugs."[7] In 1980, Ronald Reagan went right to the core of white supremacy in America and ran on states' rights, a not-so-subtle (dog whistle) appeal to racism and bigotry in working-class whites. The primary difference between Nixon and Reagan was geography and class. Nixon's "Southern strategy" concentrated mainly on the white vote in the former Confederate States, and Reagan's concentration was nationwide and across all economic classes. It was the seam that connected the various classes in white America. Reagan successfully tapped into the laden prejudices of average, everyday white Americans by associating patriotic symbols with his messages—the flag (on trucks, homes, yards, and businesses) and lapel pins (on all Republican elected officials, from the president to town council members). The flag lapel pin became so successful that on-air media personalities began wearing them, and Democrats were asked if they loved their country enough to wear the flag pins. All of a sudden, it seemed that whiteness, patriotism, nationalism, and Republicanism were all synonyms. Some became fearful that not only voting Democratic but also just being registered Democratic or Independent was somehow a sign of anti-Americanism.

In 2000, the Bush-Rove tandem took the Nixon-Reagan success to another level. This level included antigovernmental nationalism (if there is such a thing). The 9/11 attack on the Twin Towers in New York was just the ticket that W. needed to advance his brand of extreme Republicanism with a decided bent on nationalism and patriotism. This had its roots in Nixon's Southern strategy promoted by his silent majority[8] and Reagan's pro–Tenth Amendment stance. So when we string all this together, we don't have to say Southern strategy, silent majority, big government, or patriotism anymore; those phrases can be replaced by less poignant ones, such as "entitlements, affirmative action, school choice, tax and spend, and fighting them over there instead of here."

---

7   The war on drugs (aka the war on black folk) was a result of the law-and-order campaign. Pres. Richard Nixon promulgated the idea that America's number 1 problem was "drug abuse." His remedy for this scourge was more arrests, more convictions, and more incarcerations. This strategy decimated the African American community. Today they're talking about providing more funding to cure the white community of its opioid addiction problem.

8   The silent majority was a group concocted by Richard Nixon to suggest that the majority of Americans (although silent on the issues) agreed with him and his approach to law and order, crime control, and peace.

The results of the 2008 and 2012 general elections suggested that America was less gullible than she used to be. The 527s, the 501(c)(4)s, the RNC, and the McCain and Romney campaigns were unable to convince enough voting Americans to vote against their economic self-interest by voting against Barack Obama. But their defeat was not because of a lack of effort on their part. They used all the "Gs" to trick and befuddle voters, but it didn't work. They used the first "G" (God) to rally the Evangelicals and other Christian believers. And God was also used to justify their stance on same-sex marriage and abortion (gays and gestation). The second "G" (guns) wasn't used very much in these elections, mainly because the NRA had, by this time, already been very successful in Southern and mountain states where the entire political map was already deep red. But it must be mentioned that these elections took place before the massacre at Sandy Hook.

The fifth "G" (genealogy) is about race, ethnicity, and gender. It was bantered around, but it backfired. The GOP wanted desperately to use demagoguery on African Americans and Latinos to convince poor whites to support their economic policies, but it proved to be the impetus that increased voter turnout in both the African American and the Latino communities. And Representative Akin's remarks about "legitimate rape"[9] went over like a lead balloon with women.

These failures left the GOP with only one "G" to lean on—gubment (government). Gubment has become the whipping post for the GOP since Ronald Reagan's speech in 1981 when he declared that "government can't solve America's problems because government IS the problem." Of course, this was long before the banks and other businesses needed about three quarters of a trillion dollars to bail them out of the financial crisis they created and long before they seemed to realize that it was the government-built transportation systems that allowed them to transport their goods and services; it was government's protection (through rules and secured force) that allowed them to operate securely throughout this country and abroad. But still, they asked for more tax breaks, more incentives, and less regulations. In other words, they were saying, "Give me the money, get out of my way, go somewhere and sit, and shut up."

---

9 Missouri congressman Todd Akin, when asked to comment on whether a woman should be allowed to have an abortion in the case of rape or incest, he remarked that "if it were a legitimate rape, the body has a way of shutting down so she won't get pregnant." What an ignorant man! Missouri must be proud to send the likes of Todd Akin to represent them in Congress.

On Tuesday, November 6, 2012, the country held its general election for the presidency of the United States of America. Elections were also held for the full U.S. House of Representatives and one-third of the U.S. Senate, and several states held statewide elections as well. In addition to maintaining the presidency, the Democrats managed to retain the majority in the Senate. The Republicans kept control of the House and did very well in many state races for governor and state legislatures. But according to House Speaker John Boehner, "The American people want the lower house to run America" (not the upper house, the executive branch, or the courts as the Constitution prescribes). They wanted the minority in the Senate to use procedures to create gridlock in the upper house, and they wanted their media darlings and the wealthy to keep tabs on the executive branch. And they felt secure with the construct of the judicial branch.

The series *The Men Who Built America* is an iconic representation of America's economic system today, one in which a wealthy and powerful few dictate to the rest, notwithstanding the wishes or will of the people. When Vanderbilt, Carnegie, Rockefeller, and J. P. Morgan were more powerful and richer than the whole of the federal government, things were different, and everybody knew it. When, in the election of 1896, the Democrats decided to run William Jennings Bryant as their standard bearer for the presidency, the big three (Carnegie, Rockefeller, and J. P. Morgan) decided they would *buy* their own president. They chose Ohio governor William McKinley as the Republican nominee for president. They contributed a net present value of $20 million each to McKinley's campaign. Rockefeller was known to edit McKinley's speeches before he delivered them. But the Democrats had a weapon; they had *the people*. Everyone knew that Republicans were going to try to *buy* the election, but Democrats had the numbers. The Republicans' fallback position was to intimidate black Democrat voters and *distract* rank-and-file white voters with distortions, deceptions, and outright lies.[10]

In addition to being known as the Robber Barron election, the election of 1896 was also known as the *white supremacy* election. This election came on the heels of the *Plessey v. Ferguson* decision that legalized segregation by ruling that separate but equal was constitutional. This ruling would stand until 1954 when it was overturned by the landmark *Brown v. Board of Education* decision, which declared that separate but equal was unconstitutional.

---

10 Sounds familiar? It's the same strategy used today by Republicans to win races when they don't have the numbers.

During the election of 1896, Democrat and Republican ballot boxes were in different locations, guaranteeing that supervisors and other management personnel would know immediately how their workers voted. Maybe this notion is where conservative businessmen in 2012 got the idea to threaten their employees with firings or longer hours with less pay if they voted for Obama. It appears that the more things change, the more they stay the same.

How many times have you heard the words class warfare from conservatives, and how many times have you heard those same words from progressives or liberals? The count ain't even close. Class warfare is a pejorative term used primarily by conservatives when progressives or liberals make an attempt to enlighten the poor.

Conservatives have capitalized in grand fashion from class warfare, but they've cloaked their battle in distractions so as to have the victims of class warfare—the poor and the deprived—do their bidding while thinking they're fighting for "liberty, freedom, justice, democracy, and the American way."

This book will expose the attempts by the Right to deceive and confuse through distractions. There's nothing new in this book; it merely assembles available relevant data in ways not normally assembled. This book will also point out the shortcomings of the liberal and progressive elements in America's political struggles. The approach used by the Far Right might not be very nice, and they may hold the lion's share of blame for the social woes wrought by their activities, but for liberals and progressives to stand by idly and allow those you love to be deprived and harmed is inexcusable and borders on the criminal. The Far Right may be responsible for deceptions by distractions, but the Left is not without blame. The Far Right may be guilty of acts of commission, but the Left is certainly guilty of acts of omission. The *tyranny of silence* can be as devastating as malicious aggression and should be labeled a crime as well. And when it's you and yours who are doing most of the suffering, acts of omission are inexcusable, unfathomable, and outright CRAZY.

An example of the Left's omission is its failure to push through left-leaning legislation when they had the opportunity. When Barack Obama took office on January 20, 2009, 59 percent of the U.S. House of Representatives was Democratic, 60 percent of the Senate was caucusing with Democrats, and not only did they have a Democratic president sitting in the White House, but they also had a president who happened to be an African American. Instead of pushing through the programs and policies their supporters wanted, they sought "bipartisanship and compromise." Somebody should tell the Left that there's no such thing as *unilateral bipartisanship*. (It's an oxymoron.) Democrats also need to understand that compromise is a process and a method to accomplish a goal; it should not be revered as an end unto itself.

It appears that conservatives are fighting to save the rich at the expense of the rest. They're fighting to save the corporations at the expense of the country, and they're fighting to save the American way at the expense of the world. These are all dangerous notions. But more perplexing is the right wing's strategy that requires an uninformed and gullible population to remain uninformed and gullible. It also requires control of the electoral system to the extent that *enlightened[11] Americans are somehow discredited and labeled socialist, and their working-class followers find it increasingly more difficult to exercise their right to participate in electoral politics. Roadblocks, such as voter intimidation, voter suppression, and outright voter fraud, are exercised on behalf of the conservative element in our society. How long can this go on? Well, it will probably continue as long as liberals and progressives give conservatives a free ride on the critical issues that affect the daily lives of working Americans. Liberal and progressive officeholders and other leaders need to understand something about political warfare: "you can't return from battle and announce your defeat while having suffered no scratches, bruises, or loss of limbs and having a sword that's never been removed from its scabbard."*

Sometimes it appears that liberals are afraid to confront conservatives on grassroots issues like taxes. Maybe it's because liberals gave the tax issue to conservatives without a fight. And today the tax issue has become a conservative staple. When conservatives began labeling Democrats "the tax-and-spend crowd"[12] back in the early 1980s, it must have had some Velcro in it because it's still sticking to Democrats today.

---

11 Enlightened Americans are those individuals who think for themselves, question authority, and acquire their information from several different sources.

12 The tax-and-spend crowd refers to an assertion by conservatives that liberal and progressive (Democrats) want to raise taxes so they can spend more on those that are least deserving, people of color and immigrants.

Liberals need to ask conservatives if we should have taxes at all or if we should individually fund our own health care, education, transportation systems, fire departments, police, and national defense. They would soon discover that conservatives want taxes as well; their concern is who benefits from taxes paid. They don't seem to mind the purchase of a $1,400 carpenter's hammer or $1,850 for a simple commode lid. But they seem to go bonkers when they hear that an unemployed woman with four children is getting a monthly public assistance check of $365 to feed, house, and clothe her four children.

As additional evidence, I offer that during the 2009 health-care debate, conservatives consistently raised the question of how the proposed health-care plan would affect the deficit. They required that all new health-care expenditures be deficit neutral or deficit positive. Why don't liberals and progressives make the same requirement when it comes to defense spending and corporate subsidies? Sometimes I wonder if liberals and progressives are losing because conservatives are strong or because liberals and progressives are weak. Maybe it's a combination of the two. It doesn't matter how the blame is cut; the results are the same—conservatives are kicking liberals' and progressives' butts.

It's incomprehensible that those who have historically suffered the most from right-wing tyranny are the very ones rushing to the voting booths to keep them in power. Case in point: twelve of the thirteen most poverty-stricken states (West Virginia, Kentucky, Tennessee, South Carolina, Alabama, Mississippi, Louisiana, Arkansas, Oklahoma, South Dakota, North Dakota, and Montana) cast all their Electoral College votes for John McCain, the Republican candidate for president in the 2008 general election. It seems natural that those oppressed by the current economic system would be first in line to change it. Not so. They're the very ones keeping the system afloat by voting for conservative candidates, without questions or vetting. The conservative element has successfully convinced the poor that the God, guns, gays, gestation, genealogy, and gubment issues are far more important than their personal and family economic security. So how do conservatives use "distractions, distortions, deceptions, and outright lies" to snooker the poor? Let us see.

Acknowledgments

It is my pleasure to acknowledge the following individuals who played significant roles in the development and production of this book: my youngest son, Johnson Lassiter Atkinson; his fiancée, Michelle Cox; my youngest daughter, J'ne St. Cyr; my son-in-law, Bernell St. Cyr; my eldest son, Harold Valentinus Atkinson; my eldest daughter, Cheryll Elizabeth Atkinson; my sister, Brenda Ann Young; my nephews Anthony Jones, Gerald Jones, and Kevin Jones; and my devoted and lovely wife, Juju Lassiter Atkinson. But I would be totally remiss if I didn't mention the one as close to me as any other who I've previously mentioned, the one who soothed me through my writer's block and my many dispositions, my late, and faithful, pet dog, *Sophie*.

Introduction

Here's a question for people of color: if you were living in Europe under the tyrannical rule of monarchial nobility and saw no way out for you and your family, except for a thirty-day, one-way voyage to the *New World*, would you take the chance and board the ship that could change life not only for you and your immediate family but also for future generations in your bloodline? Most people I know say they wouldn't give it a second thought; they'd take everything they could bring with them on this one-way trip to the unknown—unknown but no worse than what they were experiencing in Europe.

Then there were those motivated by avarice. They generally were not of the noble class but wished they were. They had no compunction about, or problem with, nobility. Their only qualm was with the fact that they couldn't become noblemen themselves. But in the *New World*, they could get rich, become king-like, and rule just as they had been ruled over in the old world. This had the potential of becoming the Garden of Eden, the nirvana, and the heaven spoken of in scripture.

Upon arrival, they learned that this garden was already inhabited but inhabited by nonwhites who seemed to be "less than." Europeans, although grossly outnumbered, were militarily superior and, if given enough time (which the natives did), could defeat all the natives they encountered, which they eventually did. This made the *New World* the permanent possession of the Europeans if they wanted it, and they did.

The red men and brown men encountered by the Europeans had not seen muskets (called thunder sticks). They had a concept of religion and spirituality but not Christianity as practiced by the invading Europeans. So with the horse, the musket, and the Bible, Europeans conquered and resettled the Western Hemisphere for Europeans. And now that they had conquered the *New World*, it was time to make it work. Rules needed to be set, laws needed to be enforced, and order needed to be established.

Fast-forward a few hundred years, circa 1845. Whites were not only living among the reds, browns, yellows, and blacks, but they were also ruling them. There was the rule of law, and there were cultural norms that placed the white man atop the humanoid food chain, and there were cruel and brutal punishment for people of color who ran afoul of any cultural norm or law. But still, people of color didn't seem to want to adhere to the roles and positions set aside for them by white culture and law. People of color became the enemy of those who had sought nirvana in the *New World*.

The Mexicans had been defeated in the Mexican-American War of 1848.[13] Whites had carved out parcels of land to be occupied by Native American (Indian reservations). The railroads had been built and large numbers of Asians were no longer needed. The Civil War had resolved the slavery question—they thought. The slavery question didn't really go away with the Thirteenth Amendment or the surrender of General Johnston at Bennett Place in Durham, North Carolina. Slavery, white supremacy, and the dominance of Western culture and civilization were integral parts of the culture of European resettlement of the Western Hemisphere. The passage of sets of laws or the culmination of a civil war could change the hearts and souls of a people born in fear of those who look different, so post-Reconstruction America began with new laws but without the hearts and souls of those living under these laws and rules. The intent of the Thirteenth, Fourteenth, and Fifteenth Amendments and the Freedmen's Bureau Act was not generally accepted by whites

---

13　The Mexican-American War was fought over the land that America wanted that Mexico was unwilling to sell. The United States of America instigated and provoked the war, which they eventually won, and incorporated all or parts of the states of California, Nevada, Arizona, New Mexico, Utah, Wyoming, Colorado, Kansas, Oklahoma, and Texas. After the conclusion of the war, the United States gave Mexico a check for $1 million to indicate that they had legally purchased the aforementioned states.

(particularly Southern whites) in America. So we had the laws, but without physical enforcement of those laws, the intent of those laws could not be realized.

According to Thaddeus Stevens, leader of the Radical Republican Movement in 1865, "The pendulum of justice has ossified in white people—north and south—to the extent that they cannot bear to think of themselves sharing the abundant resources of this land with Negros." And here we are, over 150 years later, still dealing with a question that should have been resolved with the ratification of the Thirteenth, Fourteenth, and Fifteenth Amendments. Will white people ever carve out and accept a role on planet Earth that is less than that of ruler and overseer over all the rest? The 85 percent of the planet that is not white seems ready and willing to share (equally) this planet with their white coinhabitants, but they refuse to share the planet as a permanent underclass to the white man and his self-anointed position of "top of the humanoid food chain" and the force-feeding of Western civilization upon the rest.

So how is all this going to end? Hopefully, it won't end; it'll just change. Hopefully, the change will result in equality, peace, and harmony among the races and cultures of the world. And if it does, then that'll be the real nirvana and Garden of Eden spoken of in scripture.

Someone once asked, "If the American Civil War was a war fought to maintain slavery and if only the rich owned slaves, why did so many poor Southerners (and some Northerners) fight for the Confederate States of America? The example that seems appropriate enough is that of John Wesley Culp. John Wesley Culp was the nephew of the man for whom Culp's Hill in Gettysburg, Pennsylvania, was named. John Wesley Culp died on Culp's Hill during the Battle of Gettysburg on July 2, 1863. But Private Culp didn't die fighting for the Union, for Pennsylvania, or for his family; Wesley Culp was a *Confederate soldier*. In 1858, he left Gettysburg with his employer, C. W. Hoffman, and took a job in Virginia (now West Virginia). After relocating his carriage building and repair business to Virginia, C. W. Hoffman and his three sons joined the Virginia militia, and so did John Wesley Culp. So it's quite clear that John Wesley Culp did not own slaves but did, in fact, fight and die for the Confederate States of America and the right of white people to own black people.

There may be as many reasons for fighting the Civil War as there were soldiers who fought it, but it is also abundantly clear who stood to benefit if the Confederacy would have emerged from the war as an independent nation, totally separate from the United States of America. Slave owners, the planter elite, and white people in general would have benefited from a Confederate victory. But slave owners would have benefited most directly. While the poor, nonslaveholding John Wesley Culps of the war may have benefited culturally and socially by maintaining the legality of slavery and the accompanying disgraceful, discriminatory social system (called white supremacy), their benefits would have paled in comparison with the untold riches and godlike influence the planter elite would have wheeled throughout the South, the nation, and the world.

Even during Confederate conscription, planter elite slave owners who owned more than twenty slaves were exempt from service in the army of the Confederate States of America. Also exempt were those who could buy their way out. One could buy their way out by paying a sum of $300 or paying someone directly to be drafted in their stead. If this were the case (and it was), why then, one might ask, would poor Southerners march off to fight (many never to return) to preserve the institution of slavery? Great question and, in some respects, easily answerable. They did it because of lies, half-truths, and distractions. In short, poor white people were snookered.

Many poor whites, however, had other reasons for fighting. Many fought because they didn't want to be told what to do. Others fought to protect their homeland and way of life, and many (some say the majority of the poor) fought to preserve "white supremacy." Today some of us call it white privilege. Many were snookered into believing that without black slavery, blacks would conquer whites. Most felt that it was the natural order of things for whites to be superior to blacks. They convinced themselves that they were therefore fighting for God's will.

I begin in this manner because I feel there are still those who might wonder why poor white working-class Southerners are still snookered into voting and acting against their economic self-interest. Conservatives have made a political living from poor white working-class Southerners for over 150 years, and they ain't about to give up this "goody bag" voluntarily.

But why do so many people allow themselves to be snookered? Some say it's because the poor need something to hang their hats on. And if they can't afford a coatrack, or the parlor where it sits, much less the house that the parlor is a part of, then they find solace in their *God* and their *race*. Their intransigent attachment to the supremacy of their way of life, their nationality, and their race trumps fairness, equality, and even their personal economic plight. To them, being a God-fearing Christian, and all that it might connote (homophobic, antiabortion, and phenotypical supremacy[14]), solves their economic woes or at least gives them an excuse as to why they have economic woes. Conservative politicians understand this very well, and therefore, they fan the flames of race, rights, and taxes continuously.

The following excerpt from Thomas Edsall's *Chain Reaction* comes close to an accurate, precise position of the snookered and what keeps them snookered. In an interview at the campaign headquarters of a GOP state senator in 1988, Dan Donahue, a Chicago carpenter, explained,

> *You could classify me as a working-class Democrat, a card-carrying union member. I'm not a card-carrying Republican, yet . . . We have four or five generations of welfare mothers. And they [Democrats] say the answer to that is we need more programs. Come on . . . It's well and good we should have compassion for these people, but your compassion goes only so far. I don't mind helping, but somebody has got to help themselves, you've got to pull. When you try to pick somebody up, they have to help . . . Unfortunately, most of the people who need help in this situation are black and most of the people who are doing the helping are white . . . We [white, Cook County voters] are tired of paying for the Chicago Housing Authority, and for public housing and public transportation that we don't use . . . They hate it [the school board levy] because they are paying for black schools that aren't even educating kids, and the money is just going into the Board of Education and the teachers' union.[15]*

---

14 Phenotypical supremacy is based on what a person looks like, their personal appearance.

15 This excerpt from Chain Reaction did not fully identify the author of the piece.

There are several key issues in this statement that traditional GOP strategists generally focus on: *welfare, race, taxes, school segregation, and unions.* Republicans know full well that all they have to do is to get folk like the author to buy into just one of these issues, and he'll come along for the ride on all the rest. This is sometimes called single-issue voting. Democrats rarely do well in this arena. Conservatives fan the flames of discontent because of xenophobia, misogyny, racism, and bigotry at every turn.

And now we have another Far-Right group to be concerned with, the alt-right movement. The alt-right is a perfect fit for Far-Right politicians. They don't understand the nuances of the critical issues that affect their daily lives, and because of this, they end up voting against their economic self-interest. They are very susceptible to the Gs. But it should not be assumed that they are in and of themselves the singular reason for conservative victories. Conservatives have genuine issues that resonate well with millions in their base and several million more independents and swing voters. But there does seem to have been a chronology compiled by Thomas Byrne Edsall in his accounting of the impact of race, rights, and taxes on American politics in his national bestseller *Chain Reaction*, which suggests that the conquest of the Southern vote was not accidental or happenstance. This was a calculated frontal attack on the principles of racial equality, criminal and social justice, and fairness in America. The first G (God) was a brilliant conservative coup. The overwhelming majority of conservatives in the South are a faith-based people. They attend church, albeit a segregated church. They are Protestants, mostly Baptist, and like many readers of the Bible, they cherry-pick the King James version to suit their predispositions and ideologies.

They cherry-pick things especially relating to race—as in "justifying slavery." And when Southern white conservatives moved from the Democratic Party to the Republican Party, they took their religion with them.

Broaching the faithful in the South was not easy for Nixon in 1960, for Goldwater in 1964, or for Nixon again in 1968 and 1972, but they managed. Reagan was a little better prepared in 1980 and 1984 than was George H. W. Bush in 1988. But none of the aforementioned presidents and candidates were as shrewd, astute, and successful in harnessing God for political purposes as was George W. Bush in 2000 and 2004.

His faith-based initiatives continued, even under Pres. Barack Obama's "administration of change."

Conservative strategist seemed to have learned, early on, that attaching a strategic ideology to an existing belief structure would produce long-term positive political results. Furthermore, the God issue was and is an issue that disallows confrontation from political opponents without paying a high price with faith-based voters. Conservative strategist structured the God issue in such a way that left-leaning progressives and liberals would appear godless if they challenged conservative religious ideology.

Neither Barry Goldwater, Richard Nixon, Ronald Reagan, George H. W. Bush nor George W. Bush were not Bible-toting preachers or devout Christians in the sense that you would find them sitting in church pews every Sunday morning from eleven o'clock until one o'clock. But they managed well enough for their political strategist to sell the God issue to their followers.

But we didn't find most former presidents (regardless of party) in worship halls on Sunday morning either. In fact, there were several presidents who had no religious affiliations at all (James Madison, James Monroe, Martin Van Buren, William Henry Harrison, John Tyler, Zachary Taylor, Andrew Johnson, Ulysses S. Grant, Rutherford B. Hayes, and Chester Arthur). One might wonder how these people would perform in today's presidential primary races.

Conservatives displayed their political brilliance as they pursued the coupling of religion and conservatism. They were assisted in their quest by the silence of progressives and liberals. The Bible was scoured front to back to find the vaguest passages that might justify conservative principles on critical issues. The Bible was also used to demonize Democratic principles on critical issues.

God will be used as an integral element in political campaigns for some time to come. God will be used as long as voters believe in God and unscrupulous politicians decide to take advantage of voters' belief systems. Recently (over the past fifty years), the global trend for believers and nonbelievers has taken a decided turn in the direction of nonbelievers. This is not good for conservatives or right-wingers. If the UK, Germany, Spain, or France are credible predictors of religious behavior, the United States of America should prepare itself for less religious enthusiasm in the future.

But it was the likes of Harry Dent Sr., Lee Atwater, and Karl Rove who were the real architects of the God strategy. Dent Sr. (the father of the Southern strategy) trained Atwater from whom Karl Rove sprouted, and Karl Rove became the master builder. Never before in the history of presidential elections was God invoked as a litmus test for political association and electoral support as it was in the 2000 and 2004 general elections.

⁂

The conservative's conquest of the gun issue is strikingly interesting as well. The Second Amendment to the United States Constitution reads, "A well regulated Militia, being necessary to the security of a free State, the right of the people to keep and bear Arms, shall not be infringed." How did we get from that to selling AK-47s out of the back of an SUV? Besides being a member of the militia, most settlers in the *New World* felt they needed firearms to protect themselves and their families from animal predators, Native Americans, and enslaved persons. This was in addition to the reasons established by Colonial British overseers. But we don't have a history of collective confiscation of weapons by the government; they don't have to. In the seventeenth and eighteenth centuries, citizens' weapons were as powerful as those owned by the government. Today we can't stop the Eighty-Second Airborne Division from taking our pistols and rifles. They have heavy machine guns, tanks, and helicopter gunships backing them up. They can fire missiles from beneath the oceans or from outer space. So that story about protecting ourselves from governments trying to take our guns is just that, a *story*. And now we come to the main question: if predatory animals aren't running free on our land, and Native Americans have (for all practical purposes) been destroyed, and the slaves have been freed, who are the primary targets of our guns and rifles? Just who are we afraid of? Let me take a stab at that question. <u>We're afraid of "others."</u> Anybody who looks different, talks different, dresses different, acts different—we become automatically afraid of them. We've been told that we need guns to kill those people we're afraid of before they kill us.

Many constitutional scholars fix the root of the Second Amendment to the colonists' fear of the return of the British or the Fascist bent of the new American government. But today's personal arsenal of .22-caliber pistols, 9 mm, .357s, and even AK-47s is no match for the most sophisticated and powerful military force ever seen by mankind. Furthermore, hunters don't usually choose .22-caliber pistols, .357s, or AK-47s for hunting game. So there must be another reason for this craze of the Second Amendment. Well, what about Browning, Colt, Remington, Smith and Wesson, and Winchester? These companies' products cause countless deaths in America every day while they make billions from the death and destruction caused by their product.

So just how did conservatives capture the gun issue? First of all, they began circulating the lie that "Democrats wanted to take away guns used for hunting and home protection . . . leaving only the criminals with guns." They tied the 1968 riots to the gun issue, emphasizing it further every time a rioter was caught with a weapon (or one was planted on him). And there were many who felt they needed protection from the Black Panthers[16] should law enforcement be overrun. Democrats never adequately responded to these misconceptions and lies, thereby transforming them into de facto truth.

Many political analysts believe that because of the gun issue, the states of West Virginia, Tennessee, Kentucky, Missouri, Arkansas, Kansas, North Dakota, South Dakota, Montana, Wyoming, Idaho, and Utah all found themselves under the red column in the 2008 presidential election. In 2008 and 2012, the Electoral College totals in these states weren't enough for Republicans to win, but look what happened in November of 2016.

Log Cabin Republicans (LGBT Republicans) were not treated very well by the RNC (Republican National Committee) in 2008 and 2012, and many dropped their allegiance to the Republican National Committee and became Obama supporters. But conservatives still managed to keep the antigay evangelicals on board to balance the leakage from the Log Cabins. Conservatives have no real hard-core burning issue with homosexuality other than the religious connotations surfaced by its presence. Conservatives have to maintain their allegiance to the religious right (without which, it would be difficult for them to win). They must therefore (at least ostensibly) be antigay.

---

16 The Black Panthers was a black organization founded by Huey P. Newton and Bobby Seale. They (legally) carried shotguns and rifles. Their language was not complementary to law enforcement or the general political establishment. They were a far-left-leaning, counter-establishment organization.

The abortion issue was handmade for conservative dogma. The folk who are antichoice (yes, those same believers in the Constitution of the United States of America when in come to individuality, freedom of choice, and the right to choose) believe that the choice should be that the rest of us think like, act like, talk like, and vote like they do. Now that's real freedom of choice.

Antiabortionists have tied the notion of protection of life to their fight against *Roe v. Wade*. And still, at the same time, most of them are fervently in favor of the death penalty, using electric shock, lethal injection, and, in some cases, hangings, and the slow inhumane, miserable death caused by poverty. They're against teaching school-age children how to avoid unwanted pregnancy. On the stump, they preach abstinence but are far from practicing abstinence in their personal or family lives. They manage to tie abortion or gestation with the first G, GOD. If you're for *Roe v. Wade*, then you can't be a practicing Christian. And oh, by the way, it needs mentioning that when the first G, GOD, is discussed, the assumption is that the discussion is about the second Abrahamic religion (Christianity). The first Abrahamic religion (Judaism) is not acceptable to these evangelical right-wingers, and the third Abrahamic religion (Islam) is definitely unacceptable and should be discriminated against. Additionally, it's needless to say that they believe that all those eastern religions, and ancestral religions of Africa and the Western Hemisphere before Columbus, are nothing more than mere cults. Biblical scholars will attest to the fact that there are three Abrahamic religions (Judaism, Christianity, and Islam), not just one (Christianity). And at last count, there were well over two hundred religions in the world, and over twenty-two of them claim over five hundred thousand followers each.

The conservative evangelical wing of the Republican Party does not recognize Judaism and Islam or any religion other than Christianity. Its practice of exclusionary Christianity borders on religious bigotry and anchors their bigoted positions in other matters regarding race, ethnicity, and gender. Conservatives sold Americans on the notion that if you were a Christian, you almost certainly had to be a conservative. And if you were conservative, you should be a Republican. The syllogism here is striking.

The fifth G, GENEALOGY, was, and is used directly to motivate white working-class Southerners to associate black, female, and ethnic advantages with white male disadvantages. They want them to see race relations as a zero-sum game. They want the white underclass to feel that their rights are being eroded with every advancement of a minority group. This is the epitome of racial wedge issue fighting and class warfare. How could one who loves his country use the most disuniting and potentially dissolving issue to gain political office? How could one who claims to love America exacerbate her lingering and potentially explosive race-relation problem for political gain? No honest student of American national politics can discount the fact that race was the lynch pin that tied raw emotions with the zero-sum disinformation of race, rights, and taxes.

This all started with well-intentioned and well-meaning Democrats moving to improve the lives and conditions of those hapless souls on the bottom of the socioeconomic ladder.

It was the Democratic Party of Franklin D. Roosevelt and the New Deal that, in the 1930s and 1940s, promised clout to those at the bottom of the economic and social ladder; it was the Democratic Party that sought to shift power, wealth, and protection of the state toward the working classes; and it was a Democratic president who signed the 1941 order prohibiting discrimination in hiring by federal contractors. By 1948, black political muscle, growing opposition to segregation among white liberals, and the increased dependence of northern city political bosses on black votes produced the first Democratic convention platform to include a strong civil rights plank. That same year, Democrat Harry S. Truman issued Executive Order Number 9980, which, even while lacking enforcement authority, prohibited discrimination in all federal employment.

In 1948, one of the Democratic Party convention planks read, "The Democratic Party commits itself to continuing efforts to eradicate all racial, religious, and economic discrimination." After the reading of this plank, Strom Thurmond, then governor of South Carolina, stalked out of the convention, taking with him his own state delegation, the entire Mississippi delegation, and half of the Alabama delegation. This was the beginning of the Dixiecrat Party, later to be known as the States' Rights Party. In 1948, Thurmond ran for president under the Dixiecrat Party banner, as a staunch segregationist, and carried the states of South

Carolina, Alabama, Mississippi, and Louisiana (states that were still red even under the Barack Obama transformation election of 2008).

Also, in 2008, the country underwent a financial scare unparalleled since the Great Depression. In March of 2009, American International Group (AIG) revealed that seventy-three of its management staff would receive almost $200 million in bonuses, paid with the TARP funds received from the federal government. That's an average of over $2.75 million each for seventy-three managers who got us into this mess, and the federal government rewarded them for it. Is this the same federal government that Reagan called *the problem*? To say that there was considerable public outcry would be a gross understatement. The question becomes how does the conservative crowd—that's been making political hay by painting the government as the problem and lauding everything that big business does as good and wonderful—continue to sell that idea to Joe the plumber and Harry the mechanic? AIG is going to make it even more difficult for conservatives to sell and continue to tie all the problems of poor whites to black rights, reverse racism, high taxes, and the Democrats' attempt at redistributing America's wealth based on race. But right now, they seem to be doing a pretty good job of it.

The 2010 census revealed a new demographic population lineup regarding race and ethnicity. Hispanics have become the largest minority group in America, followed by African Americans. This new minority majority will affect funding allocations, education planning, and political strategies. By 2045, whites in America will become the minority. (They will no longer be able to determine winners of elections in, of, and by, themselves.)

The sixth G, GUBMENT, is used by conservatives as pejorative term and is tantamount to the source of all evil. Pres. Ronald Reagan proclaimed that the U.S. government *is* the problem. The right wing has demonized government for its services to, and protection of, the poor, the infirmed, and the helpless. These people are the primary prey of the rich. Conservatives, being an ally and sycophant for the rich, view all governmental actions as being injurious to the rich and powerful, excluding programs like TARP, of course.

Conservatives have managed to convince Southern poor folk that government is their enemy, that government causes their taxes to increase, and that government gives handouts to those too lazy to earn an honest living. The poor have swallowed this garbage, hook, line, and sinker. Poor unemployed folk in many Southern states have been complaining that they've heard that Obama was not only going to take away all their guns but was also going to raise payroll taxes on the unemployed. I'm waiting to see how that works out.

And now the Right is going after public educators, firefighters, police officers, and the unions that support them. Where will it end? What's next? You'll know when things have just about hit bottom when they privatize JUSTICE. They've already privatized correctional facilities; just wait until General Electric, Walmart, Bank of America, and General Motors have their own court systems.

Part I

Conservative Strategies

―――――※―――――

The solid South in the twentieth century referred to the electoral support in the Southern United States, first for the Democratic Party and then the Republican Party. Both parties took advantage of low-information white voters and convinced them that all their problems were due to the "darkies."[17] There were two prophetic comments that foretold the consequences of the 1964 Civil Rights Act, the 1965 Voting Rights Act, and their long-term effects on politics in the Southern United

―――――

17 "Darkies" is a pejorative term used to identify Africans in the antebellum South. The term preceded the "N-word," which has been used throughout the twentieth and twenty-first centuries. Post–Civil War, whites didn't have to be convinced to dislike African Americans; they had inbred hatred of Republicans, Abraham Lincoln, Yankees, and the darkies they let go. When white Southern Democrats began to leave their party and reregister as Republicans, they took their bigotry and hatred of African Americans with them.

States. The first statement was uttered by Pres. Lyndon Baines Johnson after signing the 1965 Voting Rights Act: "Boys, we've just turned the South over to the Republicans." Johnson, a Southerner himself from Texas, knew that the passage of the 1965 Voting Rights Act would become a rallying point for the anti–civil rights crowd and would allow Republicans to use race as a wedge issue in Southern and national politics for decades to come. The second statement was from Kevin Phillips, a conservative operative in the early and mid-1960s. Mr. Phillips, when asked what the Republican Party should do about all those new black votes in the South created by the 1965 Voting Rights Act, responded, "Let them go to the Democratic Party. When blacks reach a critical mass and the Democratic Party reaches its tipping point, whites all over the South will leave them and rush headlong into the waiting arms of the Republican Party." Both Pres. Lyndon Baines Johnson and Kevin Phillips were right on target, and we can see the fruition of their statements today, a half century later.

In 1968, the first presidential election after the 1965 Voting Rights Act, Richard Milhous Nixon (the Republican candidate) carried most of the South with the exception of Arkansas, Louisiana, Mississippi, Alabama, and Georgia, which was carried by a native Southern racist by the name of Gov. George Wallace and his "American Independent Party." The other Southern state not carried by Nixon was Texas, which was still strongly supportive of its native son, and Democrat, Lyndon Baines Johnson.

The Sovereignty Commission, the White Citizens' Association, the Southern Manifesto, and the Southern strategy all played significant roles in fanning the flames of injustice and intolerance for political gain. But the Southern strategy was the most successful and most productive of all the strategies and organizations used by Nixon and his operatives to win the presidential general election in 1968.

Organization	Purpose	Key People	Key Actions
White Citizens' Council	*To counter the RCNL (Regional Council of Negro Leadership)*	*Robert B. Patterson Byron De La Beckwith Trent Lott Ronald Reagan*	*The White Citizens' Council's primary weapon against the civil rights movement was economic retaliation (evictions, firings, calling in mortgages and loans, and boycotts). One of its members (Byron De La Beckwith) murdered Medgar Evans. The WCC paid his legal fees. Trent Lott took Ronald Reagan to a WCC meeting in Philadelphia, Mississippi, to begin his 1980 presidential campaign.*
Sovereignty Commission	*The Sovereignty Commission was created by the Mississippi legislature in response to the1954 Brown v. Board of Education decision. Its purpose was to "do whatever was necessary to prevent the 'forced integration' to be brought on by the Brown decision."*	*There were twelve appointees from the state legislature plus the ex-officio members, which included "the governor, lieutenant governor, speaker of the house, and attorney general."*	*The commission was funded by state taxes. This meant that African Americans were funding their own discrimination. The SC helped write "Black Codes" and paid for the defense of Klansmen with state funding.*

| Southern Manifesto | The Southern Manifesto was signed by 101 Congresspersons (U.S. House and Senate). The purpose of the manifesto was to halt and reverse the integration of public places. | Each of the former Confederate states (Alabama, Arkansas, Florida, Georgia, Louisiana, Mississippi, North Carolina, South Carolina, Tennessee, Texas, and Virginia) was signatories to the manifesto. Strom Thurmond and Richard Russell were the authors of the document, while Albert Gore Sr. and Estes Kefauver of Tennessee were the lone congressional dissenters. | The stated goal of the manifesto was to overturn the 1954 Brown decision or at least not adhere to it. |

Southern Strategy	*The overall purpose of the Southern strategy was to capture the political South for the Republican Party. One of the key planks in the overall strategy was to convince white Southern voters that their old friends (the KKK, the White Citizens' Council, the Sovereignty Commission, and the Southern Manifesto) had all relocated to the Republican Party. If this could be accomplished, they felt they could control the South for generations to come.*	*Harry Dent Sr. Kevin Phillips Richard Nixon Lee Atwater Ronald Reagan George H. W. Bush George W. Bush Karl Rove Ken Mahlman Trent Lott*	*The Southern strategy's most notable accomplishment has been the capture of the Southern vote. General Grant would have a hard time recognizing the political South today. He may think that the war had started anew and his side lost. The South is undoubtedly conservative and pro-white. Candidates seeking support from the states of the old Confederacy must bend to the racial and cultural whip if they wish to gain politically.*

Chapter I

American Democracy

"What we think we have is not necessarily what we practice"

The Greeks have been credited with creating Democracy. Whether that's true, the question now is "What kind of political system are we really practicing, and how is each major party using that system to their advantage?" American conservatives don't seem to believe that decisions by the majority are binding if they disagree with the decision of that majority. How will democracy work under these conditions?

Donald Trump said, "I could shoot someone in the middle of Fifth Avenue and not lose any votes." And many believe he was right about that. The reason he could possible do this is because Trump supporters don't back him because he's a good guy, a smart guy, a truthful guy, or even a rich guy. They're behind him because he's NOT a traditionalist, and they believe that he will keep them at the top of the food chain within their own country and throughout the world. These people aren't concerned about democracy; they want superiority and supremacy.

7

The key principles of conservatism are so very well suited for the racist element within our society that, for the most part, conservatives are labeled racist, especially by African Americans and many Latinos. Republicans have conceded that they cannot outvote Democrats, so they've decided to try and outsmart them. They've decided to gerrymander congressional districts and state legislative districts. They've packed majority-minority districts and other Democratic districts that they consider unwinnable, and they've complicated and impeded the voting process for those who historically vote against them. They pass legislation that they say is tough on crime but ends up just being tough on people of color. Street drug use was attacked with high priority, while corporate white drug users were given a pass. When the crack cocaine epidemic was ransacking the black community, the answer was "aggressive arrest, minimum sentencing, and three strikes and you're out." When heroin, meth, powered cocaine, and prescription drugs started sending too many white kids to the emergency room with overdoses, the answer was "Let's get them the medical and mental health help they need."

The black community had been devastated by punishment and criminal records resulting from drug use. Blacks were sent to long jail sentences, charged with felonies, and removed from the voting roles, while whites were given passes. Other voter-suppression methods included requiring voter's ID, moving precincts, eliminating early voting, eliminating same-day registration, and ratcheting up voter intimidation, such as falsely communicating to voters of color that they could be arrested at the voting polls if they were found to have just one unpaid parking ticket. They also hired private groups to comb the voter files to remove (purge) people from the rolls who didn't meet the prerequisites to remain on the rolls. Quite often, people of color (blacks and Hispanics) were removed from the rolls that should not have been removed. Conservatives were counting on these tactics to shore up their chances of winning in the November general election, and it did just that in 2016.

The working definition of democracy is "a system of government managed by the whole population, or all of the eligible members of a state, typically through elected representatives." Using this as a working definition, let's see how the system currently practiced by the United States of America fits and if there are some other ancillary definitions and identifiers that may be a better description of our political system than the word "democracy." First of all, the USA has never practiced pure democracy, *a form of democracy wherein there are no eligibility criterion except that of being a member of the group to be governed, and everyone has a vote but only one vote.* "Democracy is the worst form of government if you believe in racial privilege and racial supremacy."

From its beginning, the USA has had considerable eligibility conditions that authorized electoral participation. Initially, only white male property owners could vote. It seemed as if America wanted to be recognized as a democracy but craved and preferred the oligarchy that existed in Europe. In America, conservatives have always been on the side that *denied* voting rights. They were against the expansion of voting privileges to poor whites, men of color, women, and youth under twenty-one years old. And when laws were changed to recognize the voting rights of these various groups (Fifteenth, Nineteenth, and Twenty-Sixth Amendments), conservatives began voter-suppression campaigns that were second to none. And before voter suppression, there was voter intimidation. Voter intimidation could, and often did, mean violence and sometimes murder. Some of the more notorious suppressions and intimidations were *poll taxes, where selected voters (usually black voters) were assessed a tax they normally couldn't pay to qualify to vote.* The Twenty-Fourth Amendment to the U.S. Constitution outlawed poll taxes, but ingenious conservatives replaced poll taxes with other economic measures in their attempt to keep black people from voting. Requiring a photo ID in many cases could result in a cost. Relocating voting precincts could result in a cost. Disallowing early voting was a very useful tool for conservatives. When we disallow early voting, we mandate that all voting is done on the same day, making it harder for workers (especially low-wage workers) to work a full day, negotiate city traffic, and get to the polls before they closed. Taking the day off to vote was a cost that low-wage workers could not afford.

Literacy tests were administered throughout the South. Oftentimes, they were administered by individuals who could barely read themselves. These tests were administered to black would-be voters primarily, and the results were always secret and uncontestable. After the administration of the test, black college graduates, black military officers, and black businessmen were told that they were ineligible to vote because they had not passed the literacy test. Poor, uneducated whites were not required to take the literacy test, or if they did, they passed at almost a hundred percent pass rate. In the 1980s in North Carolina, Republican U.S. senator Jesse Helms's campaign sent a letter to black voters in Durham, North Carolina, who were registered as Democrats. The letter stated that "the expectations are that the coming general election will be one of the most popular in North Carolina history. We therefore suggested that voting days be split. Republicans should vote on Tuesday and Democrats should vote on Wednesday." Additionally, conservative goons were sent to black precincts with orders to question those standing in line about any outstanding warrants or parking tickets they may have and to warn them that there would be an officer at the registration table to check police records.

The United States of America has required, demanded, and forced other countries to accept democracy as their form of political governance. We've also used democracy as a pretext to outright "land grab." We've enlisted the help of the so-called *economic hit men* to arrange for the attainment of land because of country's inability to repay a debt. The repayment was never expected because the terms and agreements of the contract were constructed in such a fashion to ensure that the country in question could not repay the debt. The country was therefore offered a way out of her untenable debt.

> *Give the USA land, minerals, forest, and fishery rights in exchange for debt forgiveness. And the final condition was to allow teams of American advisors to come to their land and setup the framework for transition to a democratic form of government with branches of government similar to that of the United States of America. Once these things were in place, the country effectively belonged to the USA; with our private sector reaping the financial benefits, and our government controlling their political operations.*[18]

All the while these things are going on overseas, we're bragging to one another here at home about our *American exceptionalism*. Sometimes I wonder how we'd fair as a nation if some of our overseas actions were put to a vote here at home. I wonder if we would have voted to overthrow the democratically elected Pres. Salvador Allende in Chile and replace him with a brutal dictatorial despot named General Pinochet. And this

---

18 *Confessions of an Economic Hit Man* by John Perkins.

wasn't the only time we favored despotism over democracy. We did similar things in Guatemala, Costa Rica, Indonesia, Haiti, Iraq, Vietnam, Ecuador, Brazil, Peru, Dominican Republic, Cuba, Nicaragua, and the Philippines. We've been led to believe that we're about democracy when we're really about unbridled, predatory capitalism. It's just that democracy is much easier to sell than unbridled, predatory capitalism when you're selling to low-information poor people.

But the most disturbing thing about American democracy is the 535[19] "for sale" signs hanging from offices in the U.S. Capitol Building and U.S. Senate offices. American lawmakers are literally for sale. They appear to go along with whatever issue or position has the largest campaign contribution. And yet I contend that it's not their fault. The blame should be placed on the voters. If we allow our representatives to pretend and purport to be one thing, only to find that they're entirely something else, it's our fault if we send them back to Washington to continue the same behavior. *Fool me once, shame on you; fool me twice, shame on me; fool me more than twice, shame on the system.* It seems not to matter with some voters if the candidate keeps his word, and the reason this is true is because voters don't vote *for* candidates anymore; they vote *against* the candidates' opposition. This also explains why we see so many negative media advertisements. Opposition research has become a very lucrative business in Washington and throughout the various states. Officeholders hold no allegiance to their voters anymore. Since the passage of "Citizens United," they only hold allegiance to their mega donors.[20] This has truly become "American democracy for sale."

We have lobbyist writing checks and writing laws, both of which end up on the desk of representatives and senators who are supposed to be working for citizen John Doe, but citizen John Doe can't even get an appointment to see Representative X or Senator Y. Representatives and senators only talk to people of importance (donors and lobbyists). But they still claim to represent us, the citizens of the United States of America. Something's not right here. Anybody know what it is?

---

19 The sum of the number of voting representatives in the U.S. House of Representatives (435) and the number of U.S. Senators (100).

20 In a 5–4 ruling, the U.S. Supreme Court found that businesses and organizations could give as much as they want to political candidates of their choice. This, in effect, changed the American political system from one of, by, and for the people to one bought and controlled by big money.

Chapter II

Constructing the Modern Conservative Sell

The conservative sell began in earnest at 4:30 a.m. on April 12, 1861,[21] the beginning of the American Civil War. In 1861, there were 31 million people living in the United States of America (not counting Native Americans not taxed). Of this 31 million, 22 million resided in the Northern United States, leaving the South and the Confederacy with a mere 9 million from which to draw an army. But to make matters even worse, 4.5 million of the people who lived in the area controlled by the Confederacy were enslaved people. Because slaves weren't permitted to fight for the Confederacy until the final couple of months of the war, that left working-class whites burdened with the responsibility of taking up arms and becoming the principal wagers of war to fight for the planter class's right to continue slavery and the outlandish profits that accompanied this "peculiar institution." When the Confederacy began conscription (the draft), plantation owners who owned 20 or more slaves were exempt from service. Additionally, one could buy their way out of conscription for $300 or pay someone

---

21 Confederate general P. G. T. Beauregard gave the order to fire on Fort Sumter, which, in effect, started the American Civil War.

$300 to serve in their stead. But if the working class did not share in the outlandish profits garnered by the planters, how would the planter class convince working-class Southerners to fight and die for the planters' cause? These conditions led to the development of the first conservative sell of gargantuan proportions in the United States of America. In the middle of the twentieth century, American (one hundred years after the end of the Civil War) conservatives again fashioned a conservative sell called the Southern strategy. This strategy was used to convince working-class whites to take up the cause of the rich and powerful. And conservatives have been continuously engaged in the conservative sell strategy since then.

Before the American Civil War, Democrats were the conservative party, while Republicans (known as the abolitionist party) had its beginning in 1854 as an abolitionist party. Slavery was a $30 billion industry in the South, and yet most Southerners lived in abject poverty. This was plutocracy at its worst. Most non-slave-owning whites were subsistence farmers. They shared in none of the $30 billion annual revenue amassed by the plutocrats. And yet they volunteered by the thousands to go off and fight for the Confederacy. Why? It could be argued that the cause was "distractions" but distractions of another kind. Instead of homophobia, and abortion, they were concerned about forced racial equality and all that racial equality would bring about. They were fighting to maintain white supremacy and the way of life that was afforded them under the conditions of slavery and the resulting white supremacy. States' rights was an abstract notion that they embraced to legally justify their obstinacy. Many uttered the words Tenth Amendment[22] without ever having read the Tenth Amendment or understanding its true meaning. Yet they went off to fight Billy Yank and his *darkies*. And even now, conservatives have again convinced Americans to support causes that are diametrically opposed to their economic self-interest. In doing so, they have placed the salvation of their political party and their political ideology above the salvation of their country and this planet.

---

22 The Tenth Amendment to the U.S. Constitution is about "states' rights."

———— ⚘ ————

In 1948, the platform of the Democratic Party took on, and embraced, desegregation. This was too much for Strom Thurmond, the governor of South Carolina, to bear. Governor Thurmond left the Democratic Party and started the Dixiecrat Party and ran for the presidency under his new party banner. He carried four states (Mississippi, Alabama, Louisiana, and his home state of South Carolina). And these four states are arguably, still today, the most conservative states in the nation. So from 1948 until the present day, conservatism has constantly been sold, supported, and propelled through our political system. Conservatives, having been on the outside looking in for over forty years in the U.S. House of Representatives, developed keener fighting skills than did their somewhat "pampered" colleagues across the aisle.

It appears that Republicans have better visual acuity than their competitors, the Democrats. Democrats tend to see Americans as they would like them to be, while Republicans tend to see Americans as they are. This huge difference plays itself out in the political strategies and tactics undertaken by each party. Republicans are aware that there are many "low-information voters" in America. So Republicans think, *Why worry about where they should be? Let's just take them "where they are" and figure out the best way to communicate with them in their own words.*

Another grand strategic position implemented by conservatives is the "default victory strategy." This strategy is also called the "no third-party strategy." The no third-party strategy assumes that "if we can sufficiently denigrate the opposition (in this case, the Democratic Party candidate), people will vote for us by default." This could also be termed the *media strategy* because it is virtually impossible to implement this strategy without the media being a witting or at least an unwitting accomplice.[23] The media is aware that conservatives duck questions about their plans and agenda for the American people and replace it with steamroller criticisms of their opponent, the Democrats. The media is also aware that rarely do conservatives directly answer any question other than the ones they came prepared to answer; instead, they very skillfully pivot into their talking points. The question to the media is "Why do you ask questions that you obviously don't care if your guest answers or not?" The obvious

---

23   This also includes "social media."

answer is that the media isn't so much about information dissemination as they are about "drama" and ratings. Just in case you've been living under a rock all these years, "drama" increases ratings, and higher ratings mean more money from advertisers. And the media is in the business of making money. Conservatives seem to be fully aware of the media's stance on the issue of making money, while Democrats seem to think that the media is primarily there to disperse factual information to the people. How sad.

But through it all, conservatives are ultimately dependent on distractions, distortions, deceptions, and outright lies to serve as the glue that holds their base together. Thomas Edsall, in *Building Red America*, states that,

> *In a struggle between two numerically equal forces, the side more broadly skilled in economic combat, whose constituents control more resources; the side more accustomed to the rigors of the market, more practiced in the arts of commerce and marketing; the side with greater access to corporate power; the side more adept at risk management; the side with the means to repeatedly assemble and sustain long-lasting, powerful coalitions; the side that has revealed ruthless proficiency in winning and in shaping American institutions to its purposes; the side that has behind it most of those at the helm of the financial, technological, commercial, and information revolutions—this side has had a substantial long-term advantage.*

This depiction by Thomas Edsall is undoubtedly about the conservative side. They have unquestionable advantages in each and every category listed above. And yet they still find the need to distract, lie to, and confuse the masses by the means of wedge issues and the six Gs.

They communicate in uncommon methods. They use code words, they embellish, they misrepresent, and they lie. The most effective of these methods seem to be "dog-whistle politics." Dog-whistle politics, also known as the use of code words, is a type of political campaigning or speechmaking employing coded language that appears to mean one thing to the general population but has a different or more specific meaning for a targeted subgroup in the audience. The term is usually used pejoratively.

The term is an analogy to dog whistles built in a way that humans cannot hear them because of their high frequency, but dogs hear them very well.

The "Gs"

The Gs' primary target is lower-middle-class (or working-class) white voters. But all others are welcome as well to partake in the six Gs. The six Gs (God, guns, gays, gestation, genealogy, and gubment) are direct outgrowths of slavery, home rule, states' rights, white supremacy elections, the Sovereignty Commission, Black Codes, the White Citizens' Council, the Southern Manifesto, the Southern strategy, and the right-wing evangelical movement, which has benignly and euphemistically been termed the faith-based initiative. All these were designed to advantage racists, bigots, and intolerant xenophobes. The efficacy of the use of the six Gs is off the charts. They have worked so efficiently that Democrats are still baffled as to how to combat their success.

Democrats erroneously think that average Americans want tons of facts and figures communicated with charts and graphs and two-inch thick white papers. They seem to be unaware that low-information voters want simplistic answers to complex problems, such as seven-second sound bites and bumper sticker slogans. Just a few examples that have worked wonders lately are "Prayer Works," "Lay Off My Second Amendment," "God Didn't Make Gays," "Abortion Is Murder," "States' Rights," and "My Tax Dollars Shouldn't Go to Freeloaders." If you will notice, none of the aforementioned slogans are traditional Democratic or left-of-center slogans. Most Democratic messages and positions won't fit very well on bumper stickers; they're designed for charts, graphs, trend logs, and white papers.

Conservatives further understand that most people aren't avid supporters of *all* six Gs, but they also know that as long as they are fervent supporters of at least one of the Gs, they'll probably support the other five to get conservative candidates elected. Democrats appear to believe in the nuance approach to partisan politics (if they believe in partisan politics at all). They look upon the electorate as though they were all Rhode scholars and Phi Beta Kappas, with JDs, MDs, and PhDs. They get overly involved in the nuances of persuasive politics. In many situations, they come across as too sophisticated for the common voter. And sometimes they come across as not having the courage of their convictions. Therefore, they leave the undereducated, low-information voter to the party that *appears*[24] to understand them.

Conservatives have an unusual combination of supporters; they control the lion's share of poor, undereducated whites, and they also can boast of having the sizable share of very rich Americans of all ethnicities. It's easy to understand why the rich support Republicans, but the poor has no rational reason to vote the Republican Party ticket. Yet they're the first in line to pull the lever for the straight Republican ticket[25] every time.

And what's in it for the Grand Old Party other than winning elections? Well, they won't tell you this, but their "grand strategic plan" is the overthrow of liberalism and pure democracy in America. Conservatives see liberalism as the quintessential evil in American society, and pure democracy would allow too many "others" to vote and chart a course in American politics that would lead to wealth redistribution and a loss of overall power for rich people in general and white men in particular. They are therefore duty bound and irrevocably tethered to any and all antiliberal notions, large and small. This may explain their stance against teachers, unions, poor people, minorities, high wages, business regulations, gun control, affordable housing, Miranda rights, public defenders, trial lawyers, and just about all entitlement programs, especially Medicare, Medicaid, Social Security, SNAP, and AFDC/TANF. If these guys are against all these things, you may ask how in the world do they get people (other than rich people) to vote for them and their candidates? Here, again, they don't do it with smoke and mirrors; they do it with "distraction"—*God, guns, gays, gestation, genealogy, and gubment.*

---

24 Low-information voters, by obvious definition, are not the most discerning voters in the electorate. They are therefore "low-hanging fruit" for conservative Republicans.

25 Straight party-line voting has been outlawed in many states but still exists in others.

Chapter III

Conservatives and the Economy

$
*The eight wealthiest people on the planet have more money than half of the
people living today (3.6 billion), and 71 percent
of the 3.6 billion live on less than
$10 per day. Is it possible for protected Democracy and unabridged
predatory capitalism to coexist?*

If we envision the capitalism system as a giant pyramid, we find
the workers on the very bottom holding the whole thing together.
Atop them, we find the leisure class (people who seem to do more
entertaining than working). Atop them, we find the protector class (law
enforcement and the military). Atop them is the clergy, who cement our
belief system, and atop them are the rulers (monarchs, representatives,
and other elected officials). And at the very top is the economic system
itself. So in fact, the real ruler is the system, and some would say that's
the way it should be, but man-made systems need to be managed by man.
When the system (any system) becomes omniscience, omnipotent, and
omnipresent, man may no longer be in control.

There is no known economic model available to man that would allow employers to compete in an open labor market for a competent and skilled workforce, pay them a "livable wage," and still sell a product or service at competitive rates when competing against like businesses that pay subminimum wages, offer no workers' compensation benefits, and have no unions and no pension package. So since prevailing in the market share battle is what keeps CEOs in their jobs, paying a "livable wage" must be what gets them out of their jobs. Shameful.

The "livable wage" should include enough posttax income to afford "family needs." Family needs include, but are not limited to, "adequate housing, health care, and the ability to pay out-of-pocket medical cost. It also includes the purchase of adequate life insurance, adequate nutritional foods, clothing, acceptable home furnishings, annual family vacations, and financial wherewithal to celebrate major holidays and family annuals and create a savings account for college education, retirement, and some sort of "rainy-day fund." All these define "family needs." How many employers pay their workers enough money to acquire "family needs?"

There are a few American families currently earning enough posttax income to afford all these "family needs." But for the overwhelming clear majority of the workforce, it's a question of which of these needs will you choose to live without—"this month."

Businesses are successful at selling the workforce on this pie in the sky economic system for several reasons. They promote examples of individuals who have literally risen from "rags to riches." Of course, they don't bother to mention that for every "rags to riches" story, there are millions upon millions who've lived a life of continuous abject poverty without any reasonable hope of escape. They have us all believing that "with hard work and sacrifice,"[26] we would be the one to go from "rags to riches." We all know that it's literally impossible, under the form of capitalism we practice, for _ALL_ of us to escape abject poverty and transform our economics from rags to riches. There is no known economic model that would allow wages to be paid so that all workers become rich. So a competition ensues among workers to see who

---

26 "Hard work and sacrifice" is a phrase used by capitalist to explain why some people are wealthier than others. Of course, there are some who have worked hard and sacrificed and done very well for themselves, and there are other who have worked as hard (or harder) and sacrificed as much (or more) and ended up with far, far less than those who happen to have the right DNA.

moves up, who remains static, and who falls far, far behind. Employers want us to believe that the economic place that workers end up in is determined solely by the degree of hard work and sacrifice engaged in by the employee. But we should know that the economic place we end up in is determined by DNA, market forces, employer greed, and happenstance as much as it is by hard work and sacrifice. And needless to say, race, ethnicity, and gender play far too great a role in determining where we end up in America's capitalistic economic system.

Frank Hyman of the Southern Working Class Political Consulting group thinks that (as Mann and Ornstein's book title exclaims) *It's Even Worse Than It Looks*. Hyman proclaims, in his essay printed in Raleigh's *News and Observer*, that "Southern Republicans are being played for fools." The centerpiece of Mr. Hyman's thesis is that the Republican mantra of cutting taxes, cutting regulations, busting unions, and globalizing trade is the "high tide" that will raise all boats. But these conservative economic measures have only helped to continue the redistribution of wealth from the poor and middle class to the top 1 percent. And yet poor white flock to the polls to vote for the most conservative, right-wing Republican who happens to be running for office.

Taken one by one, it looks something like this:

Cutting Taxes

Many wage earning poor whites believe that they'd have more money if they didn't have to pay high taxes that end up in the hands of lazy, unemployed, criminal, dope users who live in the inner-city projects . . . and happen to be people of color, immigrants, and non-Christians. But the truth of the matter is that real tax cuts go to the rich (the top 1%). And it doesn't help the over-all economy as much as a direct infusion of capital at the lower end of the economic class structure would.

Cutting Regulations

They've been led to believe by the 1 percenters that government regulations prevent them from creating new jobs. Cutting regulations that require a minimum wage, and allow employees to organize and bargain collectively may be cost effective for the employer, but it would, at the same time, be devastating for the employee. This is by far, the greatest fraud upon working people. To lie to the very people you're defrauding to have them support you at the polls is the ultimate in "Hood-Winking", "Bamboozling", and "Political Deceit".

Busting Unions
They've also been led to believe that Unions are the cause of low wages and failed businesses, and are one step away from Communism.

Globalizing Trade
This is the crown jewel in their economic bamboozle façade. The one percenters have managed to convince the working poor that sending their jobs overseas will somehow help create more jobs at home. Even the Democrats got in on this one when Bill Clinton, encouraged by the DLC, decided to do whatever was necessary to keep conservatives from getting around their right flank on trade. He wasn't gonna allow NAFTA to pass without heavy Democratic backing (political speak for amendments). What the global trade supporters won't tell us is that that model of domestic capitalism isn't being practiced in America today. In the heydays of American Capitalism (the 1950's) businesses took excess profits and reinvested them into their current business or expanded their business reach across town, across the state or across the country. This meant more jobs! This meant an expanding economy! This meant progress! Today businesses use excess profits in other ways. They abandon their roles as manufacturers, and retail businesses, and become international investors. They make their IPO and move from millionaire to billionaire. And now the measurements of success have changed dramatically. The Quarterly Profit Report is the God that governs their every business move. They sell portions or all businesses, they acquire new businesses through mergers and take-overs. And when they purchase or merge with other businesses and pay

more than the business is worth, they immediately make-up for the loss by downsizing the workforce—economic legalese for firing hard working people who've been sacrificing to make the company great. This goes on, and on, and on, and some never recover from their downsizing. Some haven't repaid their student loans yet when they're force to relocate, and not only change jobs, but change careers as well. Many find themselves in situations that they're working day-to-day, living hand-to-mouth, just to get the next monthly pay check. And yet, too many of these discarded ex-employees will go to the polls and vote the straight Republican ticket, thinking that conservative businessmen are job creators, and they'll need less regulations and more money to create a new job for them. They seem to be oblivious to the fact that the extra 500 million made from selling the company (that caused you to be downsized) at an inflated price was used to expand a factory in Hong Kong, not Flint. **What will it take to wake these people up!?!?**

Infrastructure

As Philip Kotler cites in his best seller **"Confronting Capitalism"**, *"The bottom line is that a failing infrastructure cannot support a thriving economy." If this is true, and it is, then the American economy is in dire straights. The American Society of Civil Engineers (ASCE) issues an annual report card on the state of the infrastructure in the various states and the country. In its 2016 report card, the overall grade for the country was a "D". That's bad news for a country that wants to be the world leader in* **"EVERYTHING"**! *Without the proper infrastructure to support new and existing businesses, the economy cannot grow, and in the long run it will not be able to sustain and maintain and functioning economy. Here's the problem:* <u>Great projects like the Panama Canal, the Cross Continental Railroad System, the Cross Continental Highway System, and the Tennessee Valley Authority were all built by the government.</u> *In today's hyper-polarized political system, and the growing conservative Republican control of all sections of* state, local and national government, it is close to a certainty that the government won't be used again to produce major infrastructure projects. The only exception of this certainty is if the funding required to build infrastructure projects were off-set by cuts in the national budget, such as entitlement programs. I didn't bother to mention cuts in the defense department because that's the conservative's sacred cow. They'd rather die and go to hell before that cut one red cent from the bloated budget that now exist. This means that to fix our crumbling infrastructure, we must cut entitlements, or increase the deficit, or a third option (some call this the "Real Nuclear Option") which would further impoverish the poor and middle classes—**"Privatize Infrastructure"**. If we privatized the infrastructure it would bring down the entire American economy system. All cost for good and services would sky rocket because of fees charged for use of Airports, Water Ways, Railroads, and Roads. It would cost a family of four a small fortune to drive from Bangor Maine to San Diego, California, or travel by rail from Seattle to Miami, or maybe fly from Los Angeles to Chicago, to Washington, to New York. It just won't work. The solution is to make efficient and practical cut in our bloated military budget. We should start with taking those projects off the table that the generals and admirals say they don't need. These projects are the results of **"Bench Marks"**. We spend more on defense that all other nations of the world combined. There's gotta be a place for efficient and practical cuts.

"It appears that the fundamental flaw and misassumption in most lay-conservatives' positions on the economy is the notion that if we give more money to the rich, they'll spend it on building new plants here in America, thereby creating more jobs and infusing the middle class with more money. Sorry, but that train has already left the station. It used to be that way—in the golden '50's. But today when labor cost rules the roost, business is drawn where labor cost is an advantage to business, not a hindrance."[27]

---

27   *The Thom Hartmann Reader* by Thom Hartmann.

According to the Pew Research Center, "The middle class is losing ground." In 1971, 80 million adult Americans were classified as middle class, while upper and lower class combined amounted to 51.6 million. In 2015, there were 120.8 million adults classified as middle class and 121.3 million classified as upper- and lower-class adults. During this forty-four-year period, the lower class went from 9 percent to 10 percent, the middle class dropped from 62 percent to 43 percent, and the largest change saw the upper class move from 29 percent to a "whopping" 49 percent. The trend is noticeable. The lower class and upper class are getting larger, and the middle class is shrinking. *I believe it's called the hourglass economy.*

Over the past sixty to seventy years, American employers have discovered the offshore labor bonanza. So when the 1 percent got tax cuts and decided to invest in market expansion or market diversification, they used to invest across town, across the state, or maybe across the country. Not anymore. What they do now is invest where they'll have the competitive edge—*third-world labor markets.*[28] American workers can't adequately provide for themselves and their families on wages earned because employers can't pay livable wages and still be competitive in this free market system. Well, if this is true, and it is, how does the system stay afloat with millions upon millions of wage earners unable to provide for themselves and their families? It's not that workers can't provide at all; it's that they can't provide what has been promised if <u>you work hard and sacrifice</u>—a livable wage. They therefore become the *working poor.*[29]

This is ground zero in the war for conservative market share of what has become known as the base of the conservative political movement in America. These low-information, undereducated wage earners are

28 Third-world labor markets are markets characterized by low wages—wages that would be illegal in America—and unsafe working conditions, with no controls on age, working hours, or working conditions. (This is the deregulation employers seek in America.) Additionally, there's no workers' compensation, no retirement benefits, and no **UNIONS**. So why would company X invest in a plant in Detroit or Baltimore and pay American wages and be governed by American laws when they could invest in third-world country Y and sell their finished product and services at a much more competitive rate?

29 The working poor are those people who report to work every day that they're supposed to be there, work as hard as anyone else, don't complain, and make sacrifices where and when they can. With all these laudable characteristics, they're still poor, still in need of help to support their families.

the target of most, if not all, conservatives' strategies for victory in state and national elections. But how do they get them to vote against their economic self-interest? Don't the workers know that the probabilities are that they'll never be able to attain those things aforementioned, even if they *work hard and sacrifice*? Don't they know they won't be able to save enough money for retirement, a major medical procedure, four years of college at a private university, and the granddaddy of them all, become financially qualified to purchase a home? Well, how in the world do they keep them running to the polls to cast their vote for the most conservative candidate they can find? *They use DISTRACTIONS*—God, guns, gays, gestation, genealogy, and gubment. And when it comes to the "genealogy" distraction, the groundwork was laid hundreds of years ago.

In the antebellum South, poor, nonslaveholding whites were sold on a couple of issues to keep them giving their support to that "peculiar institution." For their sacrifices and their votes, they earned two things before and after the Civil War. "First, a very skinny slice of the immense Southern pie. And second, the thing that made those slim rations palatable then and now, the satisfaction of being white and knowing that blacks had no slices at all."

The economic system of choice for conservatives is "unbridled, predatory capitalism." This system preys on poor, uneducated, and otherwise vulnerable people. Capitalism, in and of itself, is not a bad economic system; it's the predation and unregulated capitalism that preys on and suffocates people. The conservative sell is predicated upon the avoidance of "rational choice theory." If voters utilized rational choice theory, poor, uneducated, and otherwise vulnerable people would vote for the candidate who would do more to further their economic cause and condition. The United States of America is a capitalistic country with heavy protections built in for wealthy citizens and businesses and less compassion for poor people and their agent, gubment.

Capitalism has been with us since the sixteenth century when it was promulgated by early Islam and spread through trade to Europe, where it took roots. Capitalism was an easy economic system for Europeans to absorb into their social and political system because of their previous practice of manorialism and agrarian capitalism. In the seventeenth century, the British, along with her new colonies in the Western

Hemisphere, began what some would call agrarian capitalism; others would call it *slavery capitalism*.[30]

Some historians wonder if slavery could have begun or lasted under a noncapitalistic economic system. If we take away the profit motive from slavery, what incentive would slave owners have had to foster such a system? The United Kingdom abolished slavery in 1833; the United States of America abolished slavery thirty-two years later. When would the system of slavery have ended under the Confederate States of America? We don't know the answer to that question, but we do know that it is unlikely that the Confederacy would have abolished the very system that they fought and died for, the system that provided the base fabric of their economic system. Alexander Stephens (vice president of the Confederate States of America) stated that he envisioned a *slavocracy* that would stretch from Anchorage to Argentina. This would encompass the entirety of the Western Hemisphere. This sounds like expansion, not abolishment.

After the invention of the cotton gin, the South turned a profit of more than $30 billion annually on cotton alone. This became an economic issue as well as a moral issue. If the Confederacy decided to do the humane and decent thing and release all enslaved persons, how would they have replaced their loss revenue?

It appears that the planter elite in the Confederacy valued profit much, much more than they valued human decency. The overarching question for policy makers of today is "Do billionaires and the one percenters of the twenty-first century still value profit over human decency?" And it appears they do. It appears that conservatives want to run all decisions, social and political, through the economic grinder and make it come out revenue positive or at least revenue neutral. If this nonsense would have prevailed during the construction of the New Deal, we wouldn't have Social Security or any meaningful infrastructure. And just think where we would be as a society today without Social Security.

But the current cloud of predatory capitalism didn't begin with Richard Nixon or Ronald Reagan. It started ninety years before Nixon's first successful run for the presidency.

---

30 "Slavery capitalism" is the economic engine that produced the largest economy the world has ever known. Unfortunately, America became "hooked" on it. After the Thirteenth Amendment abolished slavery in its legal form, it was followed by de facto slavery through segregation, discrimination, and racism.

After Reconstruction (circa 1878), many Northern Republicans began to delve into banking and other forms of uber capitalism. Many felt uncomfortable with the party being labeled a social-oriented party or the abolitionist party. They felt that too much attention was being given to African Americans and the Freedmen's Bureau Act. This was the Republican Party's first foray into the fiscal side of politics to the exclusion of the social side. It became dollars first, all else second. They believed that "a high tide raises all boats." What many of them failed to understand was the comparative wealth side of this position. The other wrongheaded position taken too often by the GOP is the notion that we're perpetually in a 1950s economy when money circulated in a community seven times before leaving it. There used to be a time when a tax break given to a businessman resulted in jobs and prosperity for poor people but no longer.

In the fifties, the world found itself recovering from World War II, and Europe and Asia were not yet attractive markets for many expansions, so businessmen invested in America. But as Europe and Asia rebounded from the devastation of World War II, those markets became attractive to American businessmen. The term "multinational corporation" became a truly functional term in American business life, which meant that American businessmen had another choice for investments. But the overseas labor market hadn't caught up with the needs of American modernization. So for a while, American businesses kept investing in American workers. But Europe and Asia caught up and even offered alternatives to the American worker. They offered no minimum wage, no child labor laws, no workers' comp, no retirement pensions, and *no unions*. This was a very attractive set of offers in that a very large part of total cost of products and services was labor cost. Companies that made decisions to keep their operations here in the United States found it difficult to compete with companies doing business overseas, mainly because of *labor cost*. So more and more American companies left America for overseas markets to reduce their labor cost and increase their overall profits. (Today conservatives try to convince us that companies leave the United States and start businesses overseas because of America's taxes on business and corporations.) The GOP was smart enough to see this, but they didn't dare go against big business (one of their most loyal supporters). They instead chose to justify their tax breaks and the need to have the freedom to start businesses wherever they chose to. This is where the GOP got in bed with big business and left the little guy behind. But if they left the little guy behind, why does the little guy still rush to the polls to cast his vote for the candidate who's taking their jobs away and increasing the price of bread? The answer to that question is simple; it's called *distractions*. The GOP has become experts at changing the narrative, exploiting the truth, and deceiving their followers. They've managed to get the very people most affected by their Draconian economic measures to be the people doing all their heavy lifting.

Some examples are breathtaking: "I hear that Obama is gonna take my tax dollars and give it to the drug users in the projects," "I don't want Social Security if it means raising someone else's taxes," "No one should be forced to have health care, even if they are destitute," "If I had a choice between owning a gun and having health care, I'd prefer the gun," "Why should my neighbor use my tax dollars for his wife to have an abortion?" "I don't want my tax dollars used to pay for a magistrate to perform same-sex weddings," and on and on it goes. So maybe now we see one of the reasons why businesses contribute so strongly to Republican campaigns. They need to keep the distractions flowing. They depend on these deceptions to help win elections. And for now, it's working.

In today's economy, the wealthy think that <u>too much is not enough</u>, so they get their *bought* congresspersons to introduce bills that would allow them to keep more of the dollars they don't need. Too many billionaires don't spend any of the new money they make. This is hurting the economy. To have hundreds of millions of dollars go into the economic black hole of malinvestments[31] is anti–economic growth. It would help the economy if they spent some of that new money to spur on the economy—create new businesses, hire more employees, and pay employees more for what they do.

We've gotta start wondering what we're all about. Are we about democracy, liberty, justice, and freedom for all, or are we just about making as much money as we can and then trying to make even more?

---

31 "Malinvestments" are investments made outside the 1950s model. Recently, these investments are made in overseas markets that don't have any positive impact on American workers.

Chapter IV

Conservatives and the Electoral Process

GROUP LEANINGS

Republican Leaning

Mormons	70%–22%
White Evangelical Protestant	68%–22%
White Southerner	55%–34%
White Men with No College Degree	54%–33%
White People in General	49%–40%
Ages 69–86	47%–43%

Democratic Leaning

Blacks	80%–11%
Asians	65%–23%
Secular	61%–25%
Postgrad Women	64%–29%
Jewish	61%–31%
Hispanic	56%–26%
Ages 18–33	51%–35%

These are groups that generally tilt or lean Republican or Democratic most of the time on most of the issues. And it's because of these leanings that it becomes easier than it should be to group, ID, and paint with "broad brushes." As it is demonstrated in the group leanings listed above, race plays a significant role in America's sociopolitical world. It also bleeds over into our economic, religious, social, and educational issues.

Democrats tend to hold an overall advantage in voter registration, but Republicans hold a decided advantage with groups that tend to have higher voter turnout performance than those groups that generally support Democrats. Mormons, white evangelical Protestants, white Southerners, white men with less than a college degree, and whites in general have higher turnout percentages than those demographic categories supporting Democrats. But Democrats hold a large majority in the demographics of the future (nonwhites and millennials). The United States's white population is expected to decline to less than 50 percent, circa 2045. And when that happens, it will have a major impact on electoral politics in the United States of America. Latinos, Asians, and African Americans are expected to exercise a considerable amount of sway on the political process, while the Republican Party's strength (whites) is expected to decline precipitously. This further suggests that Republicans need to expand their tent to include nonwhites. Unfortunately, it appears that conservatives have resorted to voter suppression, voter intimidation, and new state and local laws that would have a negative impact on those who historically vote against Republican candidates. Republicans seem to be admitting that they can't win the fair fight of electoral politics, so some think that they've decided to rig the electionscheat.

With the onset of the <u>de facto abolition of the 1965 Voting Rights Act</u>[32] by declaring section 4b of the act unconstitutional, Republicans have set out to permanently take over the political apparatus in American politics in the South. While the Left celebrated the election of the nation's first African American president, the Right planned and schemed to take over both houses of the Congress in the midterm election of 2010. This was a significant election because the census was conducted in 2010, and the congressional and legislative lines were redrawn in 2011. This process, called redistricting, takes place every ten years, and the party in power is expected to draw the lines in a manner that would have a positive impact on their party. The protection from outright fraud and overzealous overreach was to be protected by the 1965 Voting Rights Act, which required those states under the jurisdiction of the act to submit their plans to the Justice Department or a three-judge panel in Washington for *preclearance*. Republicans knew full well that now that they had a Republican Congress, a conservative-leaning Supreme Court, and no preclearance, the time to act was upon them. We don't yet know how much damage has been or will be done at the confluence of the abolition of the VRA (Voting Rights Act), the election of a Republican Congress, the presidential election of 2016, and the denial of President Obama to appoint a replacement for Justice Scalia. The jury is still out on all these things. We'll just have to wait and see. Some say we'll have to go back to the beginning to figure it all out. So let's go.

---

32 The United States Supreme Court, on June 25, 2013, ruled in the *Shelby County v. Holder* case. The court ruled in favor of Shelby County and declared that section 4b of the 1965 Voting Rights Act was, in fact, unconstitutional. Section 4b contains the jurisdiction portion of the act. It determined which states, counties, or portions thereof would be subject to the act. Section 5 of the act required the affected jurisdiction to obtain "preclearance" from the office of the U.S. attorney general or a three-judge panel in Washington, D.C., before proceeding with any changes to any voting procedure in an affected jurisdiction. Without section 4b, the preclearance of section 5 is not needed. After the Shelby ruling states and portions thereof were free to rain havoc on communities of color, especially black communities. This would further be the aim of controlling the "ol' Confederacy" for conservatives.

On August 6, 1965, Pres. Lyndon Baine Johnson signed into law the 1965 Voting Rights Act. The act was designed to increase voter participation by African Americans. Little did anyone know that the 1965 Voting Rights Act (VRA) would be the galvanizing point around which conservatives would coalesce. Conservatives began to despise the VRA for what it was attempting to do for African Americans in general and what it would do for the electoral balance of power in particular.

Many opponents of the 1965 Voting Rights Act felt that politics was a zero-sum game, and therefore, any gain by African Americans meant losses by the white majority. They fought against the VRA as hard, if not harder, than they fought against the *"Brown* decision."[33] They knew that given the power of the vote, black voters could turn back the clock to the Reconstruction era, when black votes counted, and blacks were elected to offices in large numbers. They couldn't stand the thought of blacks having equal political power with whites. Their greatest political fear was the coalition of new black voters and progressive white voters.

Although the VRA had national consequences, the South was affected more than any other region because of its very high population of African Americans, which was attributable to the high concentration of enslaved persons in the agrarian south until 1865. In Mississippi, before the Civil War, blacks actually outnumbered whites. And with the loss of life of fighting-age white men in the South, coupled with the decision by the Confederacy not to allow enslaved persons to become soldiers, blacks outnumbered whites after the war as well.

After the passage of the VRA, conservative white Southerners knew that the only way they could maintain control of their state was by criminal acts and political dysfunctions against the Constitution of the United States of America. They denied the right to vote to their fellow citizens (African Americans), and they assaulted and murdered them, all in the name of maintaining political control of their state. All states that were a part of the now defunct Confederate States of America participated in some sort of voter suppression and voter intimidation. It became necessary to pass the Twenty-Fourth Amendment in 1964 to stop former Confederate states from requiring a tax to be paid by blacks to participate in the electoral process. This was called the poll tax.

After the success of the "Southern strategy" in the 1968 presidential election, conservatives all across America began incorporating some

---

33   Refers to the *Brown v. Board of Education* decision of 1954.

parts, if not all, of the Southern strategy in their electoral politics. The most common was voter suppression and voter intimidation. They also used gerrymandering, but the most effective measure was to convince white voters that a vote cast for Democrats was tantamount to a vote cast against white people. They made up stories about black men raping white women and the government taking job away from white men and giving them to black men under the government-sponsored program called *affirmative action*. They used scare tactics about lawlessness in the inner city spilling over into the suburbs and exurbs. And they talked about taking away the guns from law-abiding white folk so they wouldn't have the means to protect themselves from the marauding hordes coming from the inner cities to take their property and their women.

Another tactic was to convince the low-information, wage-earning white worker that his taxes were too high because the government had to set taxes at extraordinarily high rates to pay for "government entitlement programs" and that these programs were set up to help black people survive because they were too lazy to work and support themselves. Mental pictures were painted that projected blacks as lazy sloths sitting around on the front porch on living room furniture, eating fried chicken, waving at cars going by, and waiting on the mailman to deliver their monthly stipend for doing nothing. They were told that these checks were to maintain lazy blacks who didn't want to work, except to work at continuing their stipend by having more out-of-wedlock children or having the government pay for the abortion if they decide not to have the child. Then there was the gay community that broke every creed of decency and divinity ever known to man. These conservative strategies may have been aimed at different groups in the electorate, but they all were aimed at convincing white working-class Southern Americans that the Republican Party was the party of and for white people.

All these issues were not thrust upon voters at the same time all the time. Conservative strategists are very smart, and they knew when and where to use which "G" to encourage the targeted voter to lean toward the conservative alternative. The overarching question has always been "What were the Democrats doing while the Republicans were taking advantage of the Southern strategy?" To many low-information, wage-earning white voters, silence means acquiescence. Besides, Democrats knew that there was still a sizable number of Blue Dog Democrats[34] that they were courting.

Democrats seem to think that they can win with just numbers alone. Republicans know they can't win the numbers game, so they play games within the game. They know who's likely to vote for Democrats, so they figure out ways to keep those people from voting. They do things like sending letters out to Democratic households, informing them that the election day has changed from Tuesday to Wednesday. They concoct false stories that paint their opponent in a bad light, and they release these stories at the eleventh hour, when their opponent doesn't have time to react, making it appear that the assertion is true.

Democrats do very little in this arena. They seem to prefer getting more people registered than do Republicans and getting them out to the polls. GOTV (getting out the vote) is not a bad strategy when it's combined with something else. GOTV alone sometimes is not enough. Democrats must have an all-encompassing strategy that does not exclude anything.

In July of 2013, the U.S. Supreme Court overturned section 4 of the 1965 Voting Rights Act. Section 4 determined which states and portions of states were covered under the act. Section 5 outlined the conditions that were to be adhered to by those covered under section 4 of the act. Without section 4, there could be no enforcement of section 5. After the 5–4 Supreme Court majority ruling that declared section 4 unconstitutional, the effect was the abolition of the 1965 Voting Rights Act. Immediately after the act had been rendered *ineffective*, several states made changes to their voting laws, knowing full well that there was nothing to keep them from gerrymandering, packing, moving precincts, requiring voter's ID, canceling same-day voter registration, and reducing time allocated to the voting process. All these new laws were obviously intended to decrease the impact that minorities (especially black voters) had on the electoral process. I think that this is in direct violation of the Fifteenth Amendment. And if the court's July 2013 ruling is to stand, the Fifteenth Amendment will surely have to be modified as well.

---

34 "Blue Dog Democrats" are conservative Democrats that have maintained their party identification although they vote for conservative issues and support many Republicans for elective office. Most of their conservative comrades have long since switched to the Republican Party.

Why is the country that wants to be known as the world's greatest democracy resorting to these tactics? Could it be that they don't believe that they can win elections fair and square and that they value election outcomes far greater than they have respect for the tenets of the electoral process that serves as the irreplaceable foundation to democracy itself?

Republicans may use these tactics to win elections and control city councils, county commissions, state legislatures, and even congressional delegations, but that won't make this country a democracy. But maybe they've known this all the time because it's not democracy that they're after. What they really want is power and control, and they don't care how they get it.

Chapter V

Conservatives and the Law

In 1865, President Lincoln and Secretary of State William Seward met on the River Queen with the "Confederate Secession Commission," which was comprised of Sen. Robert Mercer Taliaferro Hunter, Assistant Secretary of War Judge John A. Campbell, and Confederate Vice Pres. Alexander Stephens. President Lincoln wanted to discuss general surrender, but Alexander Stephens wanted to discuss conditions for defeating the Thirteenth Amendment. As far back as 1865, conservatives have been devising ways to obscure the will of the people by skirting the law, and it continues today.

Jim Crow Laws

In 1877, a national Democratic Party compromise to gain Southern support in the presidential election resulted in the government's withdrawing the last of the federal troops from the South. White Democrats had regained political power in every Southern state. These Southern, white, Democratic Redeemer governments legislated Jim Crow laws, officially segregating black people from the white population.

Jim Crow laws were state and local laws enforcing racial segregation in the Southern United States. Enacted after the Reconstruction period, these laws continued in force until 1965. They mandated de jure racial segregation in all public facilities in states of the former Confederate States of America, starting in 1890 with a "separate but equal" status for African Americans. Conditions for African Americans were consistently inferior and underfunded compared to those available to white Americans. This body of law institutionalized a number of economic, educational, and social disadvantages. De jure segregation mainly applied to the Southern states, while Northern segregation was generally de facto—patterns of housing segregation enforced by private covenants, bank lending practices, and job discrimination, including discriminatory labor union practices. Jim Crow laws mandated the segregation of public schools, public places, and public transportation, and the segregation of restrooms, restaurants, and drinking fountains for whites and blacks. The U.S. military was also segregated, as were federal workplaces, initiated in 1913 under President Woodrow Wilson. By requiring candidates to submit photos, his administration practiced racial discrimination in hiring. These Jim Crow laws followed the 1800–1866 Black Codes, which had previously restricted the civil rights and civil liberties of African Americans. Segregation of public (state-sponsored) schools was declared unconstitutional by the Supreme Court of the United States in 1954 in Brown v. Board of Education. *Generally, the remaining Jim Crow laws were overruled by the Civil Rights Act of 1964 and the Voting Rights Act of 1965, but years of action and court challenges were needed to unravel numerous means of institutional discrimination.*

The Civil Rights Act of 1964 was supposed to have been the definitive answer to the Jim Crow laws enacted by the various former Confederate states after the end of Reconstruction, but it appears to have just brought on another "tit for another tat."

Throughout America's history, conservatives have deployed repercussions or payback for actions they deemed unfavorable or *tits for tats*:

	Tit	**_Tat_**
1865–1870:	Thirteenth, Fourteenth, and Fifteenth Amendments and Reconstruction	
1877:		End of Reconstruction and Start of Jim Crow
1896:		White Supremacy Elections
1898:		Race Riot in Wilmington, North Carolina
1901:		The Red Shirts
		No African Americans in Congress
1932:	African Americans become Democrats	White Democrats become Republicans
1948:	Democratic Platform Support Desegregation	White Democrats become Republicans
1954:	*Brown v. Board of Education*	Strident Segregation
1956:	Civil Rights Movement	Southern Manifesto
	Civil Rights Movement	White Citizens' Council
	Civil Rights Movement	Sovereignty Commission
1963:	March on Washington	Escalation of Murders in the South

1964:	1964 Civil Rights Act	Sophisticated and Ingenious Segregation
1965:	1965 Voting Rights Act	Southern Strategy
1968:	Civil Rights Movement Merge with Anti-War	M. L. King and Robert Kennedy Assassinations
1971:	*Swan v. Charlotte/ Mecklenburg* (busing)	Private and Charter Schools and Vouchers
1973:	*Roe v. Wade*	Rise of the Christian Right
1980:	President Carter	Concentrated Conservatism (Reaganism)
2008:	Election of First Black President	Advancement of the "Tea Party"
2010:	Election of First Black President	Republicans Retake the U.S. House
	Election of First Black President	"Citizens United" (Corporations become People)
2011:	Election of First Black President	Extreme Gerrymandering
2012:	Reelection of Barack Obama	"Republicans Gone Wild"
2013:	Reelection of Barack Obama	*Shelby v. Holder* (Repealed Section 4 of the 1965 Voting Rights Act)
2016:	White's Perceived Devolution of Supremacy	"The Election of Donald Trump"

Part II

The Gs

Chapter I

G¹
The First "G"—GOD

Republicans have developed a three-pronged strategy in the faith-based arena: (1) They've made Christianity _exclusively_ synonymous with religion, (2) they've attempted to blot out the bold line between church and state, (3) and they're trying to demonize the whole of Islam. Additionally, they've gotten their right-wing judicial activist to look the other way when it comes to preaching politics from the pulpit (as long as they're preaching Christianity and conservatism). The GOP has benefited greatly from the Christian right. They are an integral part of the Republican national strategy to defeat Democrats and destroy liberalism. The list of propagators is long, so let's begin with one of the kingpins—Francis Schaeffer.

Because of his background and his body of work, Francis Schaeffer is considered by some to be the father of "evangelical politics."

The first G, God, is a very touchy subject that has been well used by right-wing conservatives. "If you are a believer, you should be conservative; if you are not conservative, you are not a believer." What a bunch of syllogistic hogwash!

According to a Pew Research poll taken in January of 2016, it appeared that Republican primary voters were conflicted. The poll showed that Donald Trump was leading in just about every demographic (including evangelicals), and yet Trump was seen as least religious among probable winning candidates. Go figure.

First of all, in America and, particularly, in the South, when you use the term "God," you're talking about the God of one religion (because in the minds of most Southerners, there is only one religion)—Christianity. And in the South, Christianity means Protestantism and is more defined in detail as Baptist. So when operating politically in the Bible Belt,[35] the conservative right wing ensures that there is a heavy dose of Bible talk and Baptist affiliation talk to go along with right-wing political ideology.

On this planet, there are twenty-two religions with a half-million or more followers, but there is rarely any mention of the other twenty-one by the Far-Right wing unless it's mentioned pejoratively. Nor is there very much mention of Catholicism or the various other denominations within Protestantism. But there is one faction of Protestantism that has proven to be less swayed by the Right, and that's the black Southern Baptist. And although Karl Rove managed to siphon off an extra 2 percent of the black vote in 2004 than he had in 2000 (11 percent in 2004 compared to 9 percent in 2000), about 90 percent of blacks in America vote Democratic regardless of their religious affiliation.

African Americans, as a group, are very religious people. African Americans were brought to the Americas from Africa, where there were numerous indigenous ancestral religions in addition to Judaism, Christianity, and Islam. Africans in America were not permitted to practice the religion given to them by their ancestors; they were instead force-fed Christianity (the chosen religion of the West). In the Middle East and North Africa, the prominent religion is Islam. The Far East mainly practiced Buddhism, Taoism, and Hinduism, and Native Americans were practicing indigenous and ancestral religions. So how did African Americans become so Christianized? They became that way through physical force and psychosocial cultural domination. African

---

35 The states comprising the Bible Belt are all the states of the old Confederacy plus the states of Oklahoma, Missouri, Kentucky, and West Virginia. These 15 states are highly religious, poverty-stricken, and politically very conservative. These states total 190 of the 270 Electoral College votes needed to win the presidency.

slaves initially pretended to practice Christianity to mollify their masters while secretly practicing their ancestral religions and/or planning escapes. But the deception turned into a reality of Christian worship. Apparently, the practice of deception was not passed on to following generations.

As a group (per capita), African Americans are arguably more supportive of the Christian religion than any of the other cultural worshiping groups in America. African Americans have overwhelmingly accepted the literal interpretation of the Bible without fault. One would think that this would make African Americans a primary target of those who wish to deceive the electorate by use of *distractions, distortions, and deceptions*. But African Americans are not generally the target of conservative deception hit squads; they are seen as pawns in a greater battle.[36] African Americans, in addition to being devout Christians, are also devout Democrats. Conservatives are aware that the odds of converting large number of African Americans back to the Republican Party are not very good. Their strategy has therefore been to shave and skim off slivers of the black vote, thereby depriving the Democrats of parts of their base that they had taken for granted and already counted.[37]

God and the Constitution

The first amendment to the U.S. Constitution clearly emphasizes the right to practice religion or to NOT practice religion. It also clearly forbids the government from supporting one religion over another.

Conservatives didn't invent God, but they seemed to have claimed him as their own. With the help of an all-but-submissive Democratic Party, Republicans claimed to be the Party of God. Democrats have helped Republicans by allowing Republicans to define Republicanism as being synonymous with Christianity (and lately with Judaism) to the exclusion of all other religions and the Democratic Party. No one party should be able to claim dibs on God. No one party should claim to be more righteous than all the rest. But the Republicans seem not to have received the memo on this.

---

36   The greater battle that African Americans find themselves in is the battle of race and racial supremacy.

37   Democrats go into every general election with the assumption that upward of 90 percent of all African American voters will end up in the Democratic column. They therefore don't bother to spend time in the black community, nor do they invest in persuasion advertisement.

The struggle for God began centuries ago. But this is a new phenomenon with respect to politics. In the first half of the twentieth century, there was no appreciable interparty political advantage in claiming God. This is a new wonder that seems to have beset us after the onset of the Southern strategy. The Southern strategy was created to capitalize on white Southerners' frustration with, and hatred of, the advances of the civil rights movement. All Gs were used. God was used in several ways, but the two most effective ways were citing passages in the Bible that the religious right claimed supported segregation of the races.

Conservative Dr. Bertrand Comparet offers the following scriptures to justify segregation by race:

> *EXODUS 33:16 "So shall we be separated, and all of Thy people, from all the people that are upon the face of the earth."*

> *LEVITICUS 20:24 "I am the Lord thy God, which have separated you from other people."*

> *JOSHUA 23:12–13 "If ye do in any wise go back and cleave unto the remnant of these nations, even these that remain among you, and shall make marriages with them, and go in unto them and they unto you: know for certainty that they shall be snares and traps unto you, and scourges in your sides and thorns in your eyes, until ye perish off from this good land which the Lord your God has given you."*

> *DEUTERONOMY 7:3 "NEITHER SHALT THOU MAKE MARRIAGES WITH THEM: thy daughter thou shalt not give unto his son, nor his daughter shalt thou take unto thy son."*

The other use of God seems to have been the notion that nonwhites don't have souls and that the civil rights movement was infiltrated with Communist, which, by definition, were godless people. So by playing the God card, conservatives transferred untold numbers of Democrats previously classified as "yellow-dog Democrats"[38] and other highly religious voters to the Republican side of the ledger. And less we forget, in the late 1950s and 1960s, conservatives were Southern Democrats, Democrats who were still fighting the Civil War, just on different terms, on different battlegrounds. So when Southern bigots moved from the Democratic Party to the Republican Party, they took their God with them.

But they were not through yet. In 1980, Ronald Wilson Reagan (not exactly an overly religious man himself) allowed his surrogates to woo the religious right. Ralph Reed, Jerry Falwell, Pat Robertson, Ted Haggard, and many others spearheaded the religious right movement and captured millions of Christian votes for the Republican Party. The timeline seemed to have begun in the middle part of the twentieth century. Here's how things seemed to have happened:

Timeline of the Church, God, and Politics

- **1948**—*Dixiecrat (states' rights) Party* formed as a short-lived Southern segregationist, populist, and socially conservative splinter party of the Democratic Party. A number of prominent members, Senators Strom Thurmond, Jesse Helms, and Phil Gramm, later switched parties and joined the Republican Party. They protested Harry Truman's integration of the armed forces, and they cited God as the justification for the continuation of a segregated armed forces.
- **1954**—*Brown v. Board of Education.* This decision outlawed segregation in America and, in doing so, brought about several new resistance organizations and movements, such as *the Southern Manifesto.* One of the Southern Manifesto's key supporters was the Southern church.
- **1964**—*The 1964 Civil Rights Act* prompted the defection of many Southern Democrats from the Democratic Party to the Republican Party. This act caused many white religious organizations to file for exemption from the act so as to "preserve the dignity of the segregated white church." Many states saw their applications for the establishment of private school soar.

---

38 Yellow-dog Democrats are voters who've declared that they rather vote for a yellow dog than vote for anyone **other** than a Democrat.

- **1965**—*The 1965 Voting Rights Act* removed the last vestiges of the antivoting Jim Crow era, but the white church still supported segregation and voter suppression.
- **1968 and 1972**—*The Southern strategy* of Richard Nixon's presidential campaigns exploited racial anxiety among white voters in the South, eventually leading to a realignment of the South with the Republican Party. The white church was heavily involved in the Southern strategies of 1968 and 1972.
- **1973**—*Roe v. Wade* caused the Christian right to become more vocal and organized; it also sealed traditional Roman Catholics and evangelical Protestants to the same side of a visceral issue—*abortion.*
- **1974**—Robert Grant founded the *American Christian Cause* as an effort to institutionalize the Christian right as a politically active social movement.
- **Late 1970s**—*The New Religious Right* became much more involved in politics and the *media.*
- **1979**—Jerry Falwell founded the *Moral Majority*, which was often said to be the "real" beginning of the New Christian Right movement.
- **1980**—*Washington for Jesus* was founded by John Gimenez, the pastor of Rock Church in Virginia Beach, Virginia. Pat Robertson, Jerry Falwell, Dr. William Bright, Benson Idahosa from Africa, and many other high-profile Christians marched on Washington, D.C., in an effort to support Ronald Reagan's presidential bid. This event provided a place for the Christian right to outline many of their beliefs in speeches and statements.
- **1981**—*Ronald Reagan* became president, serving two presidential terms (1981–1989). Republicans captured the Senate for the first time since 1952. Republicans meld closer with the religious right.
- **April 30, 1987**—Pat Robertson founded the *Christian Coalition*, which later became the most prominent voice in the Christian right.
- **1992**—The *Christian Coalition* produced voter guides and distributed them to conservative Christian churches.
- **2001**—George W. Bush became president as a result of overwhelming support from white evangelical voters supportive of the GOP's addition of antigay marriage ballot initiatives.

- **2004**—Randy Brinson founded *Redeem the Vote* as an evangelical counterpart to Rock the Vote as the Christian right began to take a stand on new issues.[39]
- **2008**—The Reverend Jeremiah Wright (Obama's minister) was used by the Christian right to imply that Obama was un-American.

God will be used as an integral element in political campaigns for some time to come. "God will be used in politics as long as voters believe in God."

Recently (over the past fifty years), however, the trend for believers and nonbelievers has taken a decided turn in the direction of nonbelievers. This is not good for conservatives, right-wingers, or Republicans. If the UK, Germany, Spain, or France are credible predictors of religious behavior, the United States should prepare itself for less religious enthusiasm in the future. But for now, expect the right wing to continue their religious dominance.

In state and local elections as well as federal elections, the critical issues are always touted as the fulcrum upon which the campaign will be balanced. In the 2008 elections, the Iraq War, health care, and economy were mention by likely voters as the top issues that would decide their vote. But we did not hear a lot about those critical issues; what we did hear lots about was Barack Obama's religious affiliation. Is he Muslim or Christian? And we were inundated with information about Rev. Jeremiah Wright.

Since the 1965 Voting Rights Act, conservatives have made considerable progress pushing the Gs. The first G (God) was used in the 1972, 2000, and 2004 elections. The Reverend Jerry Falwell, Ralph Reed, Pat Robertson, and Karl Rove combined to sell the American Christian world on the notion that conservatism and republicanism were godlike and those who stood against conservatism was in effect standing against God. In 2000 and 2004, Karl Rove actually enlisted the services of Falwell, Reed, and Robertson to round out the evangelical vote. Yes, God has become a political issue that we'll have to deal with for some time to come.

---

39 They begin to take issues on foreign affairs, terrorism, and presidential appointments.

During the presidential primary election of 2016, Donald Trump was seen as the least religious candidate. The top Republican candidates seen as very to somewhat religious were Ben Carson at 68 percent, Ted Cruz at 65 percent, and Marco Rubio at 61 percent. Hillary Clinton polled at 48 percent, and Bernie Sanders came in at 40 percent. Donald Trump was at the bottom with just 29 percent. So how do we explain the fact that Donald Trump received the lion's share of the evangelical vote in the primary as well as the general election?

In 2000 and 2004, we saw the Bush/Rove machine use all five Gs in concert. It was like a well-rehearsed operatic production. They combined God and gestation in places like Georgia and Virginia. Guns and genealogy were used in the mountain west, while gays and genealogy were combined in places like Pennsylvania, Missouri, and Indiana. The Gs were made into an art form by the Bush/Rove machine. In the two elections of 2000 and 2004, the distractions themselves became the critical issues. This transformation of ideas had a huge impact on Democratic Party strategists. While the Democratic Party prepared for the war in Iraq, jobs, health care, and environment, Republicans were talking directly to the voters about the Gs. The Gs are highly emotional distractions and, in some cases, nonrational distractions. That makes it exceedingly difficult to attack the distractions on their individual merits. It also appears that once a voter becomes emotionally attached to one or more of the Gs, the other *critical issues* have little or no sway in convincing them to forego their emotions and make a rational self-interested decision based on empirical data, and by the way, here is where Democrats seem to spend most of their time (trying to win the empirical data argument).

It is also worth mentioning that four of the Gs (all except guns and gubment) are anchored in the Christian faith. Now we see why the George W. Bush campaigns invested so much energy and other resources in their version of the *faith-based initiative*. The *faith-based initiative* even stole a few votes from the Democratic Party's most loyal base—African Americans. And it was the African American vote in California that helped the antigay crowd win Proposition 8. These two examples alone give great credence to the notion that "the evangelical movement in the Republican Party was, and still is, a very powerful force."

People in the movement chose the term "redemption" from Christian theology. Historian Daniel W. Stowell concludes that white Southerners appropriated the term to describe the political transformation they desired at the end of Reconstruction. This term helped unify numerous white voters and encompassed efforts to purge Southern society of its sins and to remove Radical Republican political leaders.

It also represented the birth of a new Southern society rather than a return to its antebellum predecessor. Historian Gaines M. Foster explains how the South became known as the Bible Belt by connecting this characterization with changing attitudes caused by slavery's demise. Freed from preoccupation with federal intervention over slavery, and even citing it as precedent, white Southerners joined Northerners in the national crusade to legislate morality. Viewed by some as a "bulwark of morality," the largely Protestant South took on a Bible Belt identity long before H. L. Mencken coined the term.

But God doesn't reside only in the Bible Belt. The God of Christianity has been packaged and sold in the Midwest, West, and Northeast as well. God, whether you believe in his actual existence, is here to stay in American politics. The fact that God does not show his presence in a physical form is all the more compelling for believers. Believers can thereby make God whatever they want him to be, and they do just that. Today God doesn't like abortions; yesterday he felt that blacks deserved to be slaves, and a woman's place was in the home. Tomorrow God wants marriage to be the sole domain of heterosexual adults. And less we forget, God wants us all to have a Smith and Weston.

What we have tried to describe here is the God of Abraham, the one who spawn the three Abrahamic religions (Judaism, Christianity, and Islam). Some would go further to argue that it's the only God. Well, that belief is up to you. But there is no controversy regarding the use of distractions by conservatives to corner the market on the low-information vote. Conservatives, since the end of Reconstruction, have used distractions to corner the market on the low-information vote. Even before Reconstruction, God was used to persuade and sell conservative values.

In 1820, the Missouri Compromise was all about race or genealogy. In the Compromise of 1850, the conservative Democrats of the South used race as an issue to try and give "popular sovereignty" to each new state to determine its own position regarding the issue of slavery. The end of the Mexican-American War resulted in the acquisition of more land (what is now the states of Texas, New Mexico, Arizona, Utah, Nevada, and California and portions of Wyoming, Kansas, and Oklahoma). California was admitted to the union as a free state, while Utah and New Mexico were to be admitted to the union based on "popular sovereignty." The strengthening of the Fugitive Slave Act satisfied many Southern slaveholders, and therefore, the Compromise of 1850 was supposed to be a cure all for Western expansion. But the Kansas Nebraska Act of 1854 started something that ended up being America's first Civil War.

God is such a personal entity and such an all-encompassing issue that no person, group, or political party should attempt to use it for economic or political gain. Shame on those that do. But no shame or guilt or responsibility seems to temper conservatives' bent toward "stealing religion for the Right."

Chapter II

G²
Guns

The gun issue plays very well in rural and sparely populated states, but the gun issue itself does not deliver the Electoral College votes in great quantity. The gun issue is closely related to the genealogy issue. There is a closely aligned race and ethnicity piece associated with guns and genealogy. Conservatives play this card very well. In the South and Northwest, conservatives use hunting as the snare to catch voters, and in the urban and suburban areas, they fight against gun control and fight for home and personal protection. The underlying assumption is that when the police, Army National Guard, Army Reserve, and regular army can't stop the rioting hoards from the inner city, everybody will need their own personal weapons for self and family protection. But that's a lie; the real compelling issue before Heller[40] and McDonald[41] was the gun manufacturers' inability to sell guns in highly populated markets like Chicago, Philadelphia, New York, Washington, and Los Angeles. When one of these cities passed gun-control laws, gun manufacturers saw millions and millions of dollars fly out the window. Gun manufacturers don't appear to care about home protection, gun control, or self-defense; it appears that their number 1 concern is the SELL of guns. "I think they just wanna make money, and they don't want potential lucrative markets closed off from them just to make communities and cities more safe."

To understand America's fixation with guns, one has to first understand Americas' origin. What is now known as the Americas was home to "red, brown, and black" people prior to 1492. The Europeans' first reaction to the Americas was WOW! They were understandably excited over the new species of plants and animals never before seen by Europeans. So on their return trip to Europe, that brought samples of plants and animals from the *New World*. Many Europeans were excited about the possibilities of new food sources and the beginning of new medicines and other life products. But there were also those who only saw the wealth and riches that the *New World* could provide. Initially, the novelty of the cross-cultural experiences was enough to keep the peace between the Europeans and the natives, but pretty soon, the desire for wealth and riches was too powerful for Europeans to suppress. The native population began to see their rituals and customs disrespected, their wishes and request ignored, and their women assaulted. When the natives began to defend their property rights, Europeans saw this as "savage aggression" and therefore felt they were justified in anything they could do to protect *themselves. I sometime wonder if Europeans would have seen themselves as savages had they stayed home and defended their culture against an invading culture from parts unknown.* Nonetheless, they saw the natives of the Americas as nothing more than savage beast. They therefore felt they were justified in doing whatever was necessary to survive in this rich new land, even if it meant genocide. The Europeans were terrified of the

---

40 The U.S. Supreme Court ruled in Washington, D.C. v. Heller that individual citizens had a right to keep and bear arms unconnected with the militia provisions of the 2nd Amendment.

41 The Court also held in the McDonald v. Chicago decision that the Heller decision applied to the states as well protected by the "Equal Protection Clause" of the 14th Amendment.

possibility of attacks by natives. They couldn't image life without weapons to defend themselves. Weapons became a fact and way of life.

When the British set up their colonies, the farmer, the militia, and the British soldiers all had the same weaponthe flintlock musket. So to control the colonist, British soldiers had to confiscate the weapons of the colonist, leaving them vulnerable to attack from the natives as well as the British. When the colonist became members of the United States of America, they wanted to ensure that they had weapons to protect themselves from attack by the natives *and* their government. This was the pretext for the Second Amendment to the Constitution. But as was earlier stated, "The farmer, the militia, and the British soldiers all had the same weapon." That's far from the case today. Today's long guns and handguns owned by Americans are no match for the tanks, missiles, and drones the military possesses today. So the Second Amendment as written doesn't hold true for the circumstances of modern America. If it did, shouldn't Americans belonging to National Guard units (under the protection of the militia implications) be able to own APCs[42] and armed helicopters? The purpose for gun ownership purported by most Americans is "hunting, sporting, and personal and home protection." The first two reasons are newly born reasons, created here in America, but the issue of personal and home protection is born straight out of early Europeans' fear of the natives. And today native means anybody who ain't *white*. Gun ownership has therefore morphed into an integral part of the racial issue in America, which means that it's gonna be difficult to solve one without solving the other.

No one should underestimate conservative strategists' ability to manage their demographics. They seem to use the results of crosstab surveys much more effectively than do liberals and progressives. For example, they know that survey respondents who answer affirmatively to questions about gun ownership and being tough on immigration are likely to back tough police tactics, less likely to support issues favorable to minorities, and ultimately support conservative judges and extreme right-wing political candidates. This means that you don't have to ask these guys what they think about abortion, the LGBT community, or taxes; it's a no-brainer that if the aforementioned crosstabs are positive, *the other variables don't matter.*

---

42 APCs are "armored personnel carriers" used by the military to transport soldiers in a safe manner when confronting small-arms fire.

An example in recent political history would be Donald Trump's response to the request that he release his tax return. Trump's response was "My supporters don't care about my tax returns and don't want to see them." Trump knows that key crosstab responses indicate that his supporters have already been sold on immigration, Muslims, Hispanics, African Americans, women, and political correctness, and as long as he holds steady on those positions, his supporters will go along with his positions on just about anything else (bringing in again Trump's statement we've mentioned throughout this book, and I repeat, "I could shoot someone in the middle of Fifth Avenue in New York City and wouldn't lose any votes.")

And now it should become a little clearer why the NRA (National Rifle Association) endorsed Donald Trump in the 2016 general election for president.

The figure on the following page tends to explain why Republicans support gun ownership issues. It appears that older white Southern males are the primary gun owners in the country. Crosstabs will also show that these older white Southern males are also evangelical Christians, anti-LGBT, pro-life, monocultural assimilationist, and advocates of a business-friendly federal government.

Second Amendment to the United States Constitution

"A well-regulated Militia, being necessary to the security of a free State, the right of the people to keep and bear Arms, shall not be infringed."

It is abundantly clear that the intent of the Second Amendment was the same as was the others listed in the Bill of Rights. They were intended to ensure that the misdeeds and tyrannical acts committed by the British would never be repeated on Americans by the British or by any other government again. This meant that the framers were concerned that they would give power to a government that would later misuse that power by taking guns away from citizen before attacking them, thereby leaving them defenseless. The standard military armament in the eighteenth century was muskets, cannons, and pistols. If citizens were allowed to keep and bear these arms, they would have the power to hold off, even destroy, government troops.

The United States Bill of Rights, found by the U.S. Supreme Court, in District of Columbia v. Heller (June 26, 2008),

> to protect the pre-existing individual right to possess and carry weapons (i.e., "keep and bear arms") in case of confrontation is paramount. Codification of the right to keep and bear arms into the Bill of Rights was influenced by a fear that the federal government would disarm the people in order to impose rule through a standing army or select militia, since history had shown that taking away the people's arms and making it an offense for people to keep them was the way tyrants eliminated resistance to suppression of political opponents.[43]

Before the *Heller* decision, there was much disagreement as to whether it protected a collective right or an individual right because the amendment contains a prefatory clause that refers to a "well-regulated militia." Previously, the Supreme Court had not directly addressed the amendment or had only done so in limited or ambiguous terms.

A minority has argued that because the District of Columbia, which is not a state, was the only government involved in *Heller*, uncertainty remains concerning whether the Second Amendment applies to state and local jurisdictions by way of incorporation through the Fourteenth Amendment. However, the court's unambiguous declaration that the right to bear arms is an individual privilege, taken with the Fourteenth Amendment's clear stricture that "no state shall make or enforce any law which shall abridge the privileges or immunities of citizens of the United States," appears to conclusively support incorporation.

The conservative right supports guns because rural Americans want guns for protection when the militia (local and state police and the National Guard) ain't there. Oh, and did I mention that American gun manufactures make tons of money selling guns and that some of the proceeds from gun sales end up as contributions to the campaigns of candidates of the conservative right? This arms merry-go-round has many benefits. First, conservative congresspersons receive campaign contributions from the gun lobby, and second, conservative congresspersons cast votes to protect the gun lobby by ensuring that citizen are able to purchase as many guns as they desire (for whatever purpose they choose). Gun manufacturers then sell more guns and make

---

43 *Reducing Gun Violence in America*, edited by Daniel W. Webster and Jon S. Vernick with foreword by Mayor Michael R. Bloomberg, 2013.

more money to give to the people's representatives, who, in turn, vote in favor of the gun lobby again. And around, and around, and around we go!

The National Rifle Association (NRA)

The NRA is recognized by some as the most powerful lobbying organization in Washington. In 1871, William Conant Church and George Wood Wingate established the American Rifle Association, which would later become the National Rifle Association (NRA). The NRA touts itself as a "nonprofit, nonpartisan" organization with a 501(c)(4) tax cover. And yet the NRA makes enough profit to pay its CEO, Wayne LaPierre, over $1 million annually and contribute handsomely to the election and reelection campaigns of scores of conservative congresspersons. The NRA claims to be nonpartisan but has a reputation for backing conservative Republicans for office, even threatening them with primary opposition if they don't yield to their demands. The NRA's cozy relationship with gun manufacturers and conservative lawmakers is obvious and easily understandable. Gun manufacturers make profits from selling guns; they, in turn, use those profits to make donations to the NRA. And now they'll also be able to get directly involved with political campaigns because of the Robert's court ruling—"Citizens United"— that classified businesses as individuals and allowed them to make unlimited contributions to affect the outcome of political races. These donations to the NRA, and now indirectly to campaigns, constitute the second dot to be connected. The third dot is the elected officials who have benefited from NRA and gun manufacturers donations, casting vote that are favorable to the gun manufacturers' ability to continue polluting American cities and homes with countless weapons designed for one primary reason, to kill men, women, and children.

The NRA is without question the most powerful, most successful lobbying organization on Capitol Hill. They've become so powerful that they're now proliferating their services to include other non-gun-related issues, such as education and labor. But the crux of their political involvement is to convince voters that those who would support legislation to control guns are, in fact, trying to take away the right to bear arms and thereby destroying the Second Amendment. Some NRA supporters advocated the notion that Pres. Barack Obama was going to repeal the Second Amendment. *How ridiculous can you get?* Anyone with even a quaint understanding of the American Constitution knows that a president cannot unilaterally make changes to the Constitution. And yet the NRA and the gun manufacturers continue to make these falsehoods a centerpiece of their rhetoric to distract and deceive the voters through distortions and outright lies.

In the gun states of Alaska, Louisiana, Wyoming, Arizona, Mississippi, Arkansas, Alabama, Tennessee, West Virginia, Montana, South Carolina, Georgia, Kentucky, Oklahoma, Missouri, and Idaho, conservative victory is almost assured. All the aforementioned states voted for John McCain in 2008. In 2012, twelve of the sixteen states have Republican governors, and twelve of the sixteen states have Republican-controlled state legislature. West Virginia and Kentucky are two interesting states in that they both have Democratic governors and Democratic-controlled state legislatures but voted for the Republican candidate for president.

Firearm Deaths Per One Hundred Thousand Residents

There were 17 of the top 19 firearm death states voted for the Republican presidential candidate in 2012 and supported the NRA and gun manufacturers.

"They voted to keep killing their fellow citizens, not foreign invaders or gubment agents (as the Second Amendment was initially designed to do), but they're killing their fellow citizens, and they keep putting folks in office who would allow the NRA and the gun manufacturers to put more and more guns on the streets so Americans can kill more of their fellow citizens."

Rank	States	No. Gun Deaths Per 100,000 Citizens	Party Voted for in 2012 Presidential Election
1	**Alaska:**	20.0	*Republican*
2	**Louisiana:**	19.5	*Republican*
3	**Wyoming:**	18.8	*Republican*
4	**Arizona:**	18.0	*Republican*
5	**Nevada:**	17.3	*Democrat*
6	**Mississippi:**	17.3	*Republican*

7	New Mexico:	16.6	*Democrat*
8	Arkansas:	16.3	*Republican*
9	Alabama:	16.2	*Republican*
10	Tennessee:	15.4	*Republican*
11	West Virginia:	14.7	*Republican*
12	Montana:	14.5	*Republican*
13	South Carolina:	13.8	*Republican*
14	North Carolina:	13.6	*Republican*
15	Georgia:	13.4	*Republican*
16	Kentucky:	13.1	*Republican*
17	Oklahoma:	13.1	*Republican*
18	Missouri:	12.3	*Republican*
19	Idaho:	12.3	*Republican*

The chart listed above illustrates the connection among the NRA, gun manufacturers, most Southern states, the Republican Party, and gun deaths per capita. Conservative strategists look for commonalities to exploit in garnering support for their right-wing ideology. Now it's "God, guns, gays, gestation, genealogy, and gubment.

The NRA is not *officially* a subsidiary of gun manufacturers, but it's close to it. The relationship among gun manufacturers, the NRA, and the United States Congress is pathetic, if not criminal. It's like selling drugs on the White House lawn, it's like setting up prostitution in the chambers of the Supreme Court, and it's like selling child porn movies at the Lincoln Memorial.

They don't seem to care that people are watching, that people know what they're doing and why they're doing it. This vicious circle of gun manufacturers funding the NRA, and the NRA making campaign contributions to representatives and senators, and representatives and senators voting to keep gun sales safe for manufacturers is abhorrently evil. And the greatest violation of all is when members of Congress allow the NRA to write legislation favorable to the gun manufacturers and congresspersons sign the bill as though it were *their* brainchild.

How many more innocent adults and children have to die before the voters in this country wake up to what's going on around them? How many more mass shootings have to take place before citizens get enough backbone to strike back by refusing to vote for the NRAs, gun manufacturers, and their sycophants in the U.S. Congress? We must fight back because what we're really fighting for is that mother or that child (that could be your own) yet to be senselessly gunned down by someone using a weapon that shouldn't have been legally sold in America.

Just what should and can be done about the NRA? First, let's look at the NRA. What is it? Who runs it? To whom is it responsible? Who are the primary beneficiaries from the NRA's actions?

The National Rifle Association is a tax-exempt, fire-breathing, swashbuckling, uncompromising beast. The NRA was ostensibly formed as a rifle club to help members become better sharpshooters. Some of its earlier affiliations were with organizations, such as Boy Scouts of America and the 4-H Club. But the gun juggernaut known today as the NRA is much, much more than a marksmanship club or a social club for kids. Today's NRA, which started as a Second Amendment protection organization, has blossomed into the country's most feared and most effective lobbying machine in Washington.

The NRA once made its bones by convincing prospective supporters that pro-government liberals wanted to take their guns away, leaving the criminal element alone as the only armed segment of American society. But now the NRA's tentacles stretch from the Second Amendment to the First Amendment, where you'll find it on both sides of the free speech issue. It appears that the NRA is for the exercise of free speech for corporations through campaign contributions from businesses but against free speech for Occupy Wall Street demonstrators while they're protesting against banks and big business. Because of their stance on the Second Amendment, you'd think that they'd be on the side that forbids unusual searches described in the Fourth Amendment, but they're not. On Fourth Amendment issues, the NRA finds itself siding with other conservatives on the side of law enforcement that allow for stop-and-frisk search and seizures because it's the proper conservative, alt-right, racial, urban thing to do. And they're definitely for the Tenth Amendment and the conservative interpretation regarding "states' rights." So it should be no surprise that very few people of color support the NRA.[44]

---

44 The NRA has very few African American members. They won't divulge exactly how many African American members they have, but by all indicators (convention attendance), even as gun purchases by African Americans are on the rise, African American membership in the NRA is very, very low. African

The NRA is the most powerful lobbying firm in Washington. They are the group that incumbents fear most. What kind of democracy do we have when our representative fear the NRA more than they fear *our* votes? As Mr. Wolin would title it, it's "democracy incorporated." Some would just say it's "democracy for sale." Whatever it is, it's far from what the framers had in mind when they spoke of one man, one vote. The NRA and other lobbying organizations may have only one vote, but it's the loudest vote and therefore the most powerful vote in the room. It's the vote in the room that representatives listen to first and foremost.

The National Rifle Association has money, motivated members, and powerful allies in Congress. But what puts the NRA in a separate class among interest groups is its track record of defeating incumbents. In Washington, that's real power. Thus, calls for new gun-control measures after the Virginia Tech shootings, even after Sandy Hook, faced a difficult path on Capitol Hill.

The National Rifle Association generally has kept a low profile in the days since the Tucson, Arizona, shooting rampage that killed six and wounded fourteen, including Rep. Gabrielle Giffords. But the group has begun to push back at congressional proposals to tighten gun laws, warning lawmakers not to chip away at gun rights.

"Even while our country was respecting the heartache of the people of Tucson and waiting for the full facts of the case, anti-gun activists were renewing their push for more gun control laws," said Chris W. Cox, executive director of the NRA Institute for Legislative Action, in a Wednesday letter to members of Congress. "Indeed, gun control advocates were quick to push several schemes," Cox said. Cox was particularly critical of a joint proposal by Sen. Frank R. Lautenberg of New Jersey and Rep. Carolyn McCarthy of New York, both Democrats, to bar the manufacture and sale of high-capacity ammunition clips like the one used by Arizona shooting suspect Jared Loughner. "These magazines are standard equipment for self-defense handguns and other firearms owned by tens of millions of Americans," Cox wrote. Cox also called out Republican Rep. Peter King of New York for his plan to ban

---

Americans have established their own gun organization—"National African American Gun Association." NAAGA was established on February 28, 2015, in honor of Black History Month. Their current president is Phillip Smith, a graduate of UC Davis.

firearms within one thousand feet of members of Congress and other high-ranking federal officials.

"Obviously, this proposal would be ignored by anyone who intends to harm a government official," he said. "But it would impose extraordinary burdens on honest gun owners, creating potentially hundreds of square miles of roving 'gun free' areas throughout the United States."

The gun industry and the National Rifle Association (NRA) don't want you to know that gun sales have stagnated for years, and their campaigns to legalize concealed carry and fight restrictions on the sales of highly lethal weapons are part of their strategy to boost stagnant gun sales.

There may never be a time in America when there are no guns. There may never be a time in America when the murder rate is nil, but that doesn't mean we shouldn't *attempt* to attain that goal.

George Zimmerman, Trayvon Martin

In 2012, George Zimmerman shot and killed Trayvon Martin. George is a white Hispanic; Trayvon was an African American. George was armed with a 9-mm handgun; Trayvon was armed with a pack of Skittles candy and a can of ice tea. Because of Florida's "stand-your-ground law," George was not charged or arrested. Police said they didn't have enough evidence to refute George's account of the shooting. Besides the obvious distain for the police action or, in this case, inaction, questions are raised regarding the origin and purpose of the "stand-your-ground law." It appears that Florida's law allows a person beset by fear to stalk a person whom they are afraid of and shoot them down in cold blood because the armed person doing the stalking is afraid of the unarmed person being stalked. It doesn't make a lot of sense, does it?

It should be first understood that the city of Sanford or the state of Florida was not responsible for the origin of this law. This law was the brainchild of the National Rifle Association (NRA). Why, one might ask, would the NRA be interested in a law that gives citizen the right to use deadly force *IF* they believe that their lives may be in danger? Well, it has been documented that wherever the law has been instituted, gun sales rose precipitously. Additionally, law enforcement officials generally feel that an armed citizenry with the law behind them might make criminals think twice before they violate the public's law-and-order edicts. All this is highly problematic. The NRA has never been elected to any office, and yet they have more power than most elected officials. And because they're not elected officials, they're beyond our management and control. But they're not beyond the control of our purchasing power, nor are they beyond the control of the Congressmen whom they give campaign contributions.

Our latest census revealed that we have over three hundred million people living in the United States of America, and there are over three hundred million guns in America. So I guess a boycott of the gun industry by gun-control advocates wouldn't be that successful. The obvious question is "What then can be done about the NRA's sway on our elected officials?" The answer is simple: pressure your elected officials. Just as ALEC[45] had to make some adjustments when some of their key sponsors terminated or threatened to terminate their contract because of ALEC's stance on critical social issues that their sponsor's clients were concerned about, voters can bring pressure to bear on congresspersons who cater to the NRA's every wish and command.

The NRA has become the most powerful lobbying organization in the country, and their power reaches far, far beyond gun issues. The NRA has weighed in on conservative public education issues. What's next, abortion and gay rights? Don't be surprised to see an NRA ad soon supporting Congressman X or defaming Congressman Y because of the stance on issues like abortion and/or gay rights.

James Holmes in Aurora, Colorado, and Wade Michael Page in Milwaukee, Wisconsin, both committed horrible acts with guns. Had the NRA been less successful over the years, these two men may not have been able to commit such heinous acts. In Colorado, Mr. Holmes killed sixteen people in a crowded theater; Mr. Page killed several people in a Sikh temple. Both crimes appear to have been committed by deranged people, but without the help of an insane gun laws, many of those now dead may have been saved. And yet we continue to send legislators to Congress who are afraid of the NRA and the gun manufacturers they represent to the extent that they allow the enactment of legislation to continue the profits and deaths caused by guns. When will there be a candidate running on a platform of gun control who'll have a chance to win despite the mega-millions contributed to his opponent by the NRA? When will the public decide to vote for the NRA's opponent?

---

45   The "American Legislative Exchange Council" is a conservative control unit that has become highly successful at getting conservatives elected and reelected and keeping conservative thought in main stream media.

Are we terminally afraid of the NRA? If we are, we need to reexamine our commitment to the *true* meaning of democracy, freedom, justice, equality, fairness, and the American way.

There are five countries that don't allow their law enforcement officials to carry firearms (Britain, Ireland, Norway, Iceland, and New Zealand). All five of these countries have far less crime rates than the United States of America does, and their police safety hazard rates are considerably lower than that of the United States. Yet there is no serious consideration being given to disarming the police when police officers have been charged, or not been charged, and, in a very few cases, even convicted of the murder of unarmed American citizens.

And Many, Many Others

Tamir Rice—Clevland, Ohio
William Chapman—Portsmouth, Virginia
John Crawford—Beavercreek, Ohio
India Kager—Virginia Beach, Virginia
Eric Harris—Tulsa, Oklahoma
Sandra Bland—Waller Country, Texas
Victor White—Iberia Parrish, Louisiana
Alton Sterling—Baton Rouge, Louisiana
Philando Castille—Falcon Heights (suburb of St. Paul), Minnesota

One has to wonder if Eric, Walter, and Michael would still be with us today if we had law enforcement policies similar to those of the five countries aforementioned that don't have armed police officers.

Sandy Hook Elementary School Shooting

On December 14, 2012, Adam Lanza, twenty, fatally shot twenty children and six adult staff members and wounded two at Sandy Hook Elementary School in the village of Sandy Hook in the town of Newtown, Connecticut. Before driving to the school, Lanza had shot and killed his mother, Nancy Lanza, at their Newtown home. After killing students and staff members, Lanza committed suicide by shooting himself in the head as first responders arrived.

The massacre was the second deadliest school shooting in the United States's history after the 2007 Virginia Tech massacre. It also was the second deadliest mass murder at an American elementary school after the 1927 Bath School bombings in Michigan.[46]

Words have been difficult to come by to describe the shock and horror felt by all. Pres. Barack Obama fought back tears as he addressed a mournful nation after the senseless attack. Gun-control advocates seized upon the situation to call for greater gun control and more regulations on the unbelievable proliferation of gun in America. We have roughly one gun for every man, woman, and child in America, over three hundred million and counting. But no matter how many children get riddled with rounds from high-powered rifles or semiautomatic handguns, the NRA, the gun manufacturers, and conservative congresspersons continue to reject any notion to control guns in America.

Why don't we try a different approach? Why not seek to control the ammunition supply? If we could somehow stamp, emboss, bar code, or otherwise identify every bullet and bullet casing, this would be a tremendous help to forensic detectives in police departments all over America, and it would have an impact on people showing up at public places armed to the teeth with literally hundreds of rounds of ammunition. What about limiting the numbers of rounds one is able to purchase (based on what his needs are and how many he's used since his last purchase)? Why, for example, would a homeowner need more than a couple of extra clips of ammo for a weapon used for home protection? Why would a hunter who is limited to a previously set number of game he's allowed to shoot need one hundred or more rounds of ammo during his hunting trip? And why would a gun enthusiast or collector need hundreds of rounds of ammo on hand? Why couldn't public and private firing ranges carry enough ammo so customers could purchase their ammo at the firing ranges? All these questions have the same answer. And the answer is *the real reason many of these gun owners want guns is to protect themselves against a government (even their own) or protect themselves from the hordes that might descend upon them from the inner cities to take their properties, ravish their wives and daughters, and enslave them and their sons.*

---

46 Andrew Kehoe was a fifty-five-year-old farmer in town of Bath, Michigan, in 1927. In 1926, his farm was foreclosed on; in 1927, his was defeated for his job as town treasurer; and his wife was about to leave him. He bombed the schoolhouse and his farm and killed his wife and himself. At this time, this was the largest mass murder in the country ever.

In 1791, when the Bill of Rights, including the Second Amendment, was adopted, the muskets carried by the average homeowner was as powerful and sophisticated as the latest musket carried by the British or the American armies. So the original intent of the Second Amendment has no bearing on the reason Americans want guns today. And by the way, hunters don't use .50-caliber machine guns to hunt rabbit and quail. These high-powered, hyper-deadly weapons have but one use: to kill as many human beings as possible in the shortest period possible.

If we didn't act in the face of Sandy Hook where dozens of children were murdered unnecessarily, when are we going to act? Why do we continue *begging* the NRA and gun manufacturers to see it our way while many more continue to die? Are we not strong enough? Do we not have the will to protect our greatest possessions—our children? It's time to stop playing games with the NRA, the gun manufacturers, and the crony congressperson whom they've purchased. It's time to take the matter of gun control into our own hands and act as if the lives of our love ones depend on it because they do.

There were forty-nine killed in Orlando, Florida, and five police officers killed in Dallas, Texas. Both mass murders were caused, in part, by deranged people being able to access lethal weapons at will. To quote President Obama, "We need to make it harder for these people to get their hands on lethal weapons."

Chapter III

G³
Gays
(LGBTQ)
Lesbian, Gay, Bisexual, Transgender,
and Queer Americans

Lesbian, gay, bisexual, and transgender Americans have been maligned (rightly or wrongly) since the beginning of this country and for millennia prior to the birth of these United States of America.

Conservatives have used the gay issue to spread its influence among the Christian right. They construct a political sell that equates homosexuality with ungodliness. They use excerpts from the Bible to justify hatred of homosexuals. But hypocritically, they engage in homosexual acts and allow the homosexual act of those close to them as long as they share their general political beliefs. Conservatives have managed to tie homosexuality, atheism, gun control, un-Americanism, people of color, liberalism, government, and democrats all together in a single knot and labeled it "wrong." Many have brought into this crazy notion and made their sentiments known at the polls. Still, many others are discerning enough to be against, or be for, one of the aforementioned without being syllogistically linked to them all.

The amazing thing about all this is the hypocrisy of it all. Many of the most ardent defenders of heterosexuality and proclaimed enemies of homosexuality are, in fact, homosexuals themselves.

Antigay Activists Caught Being Gay

Here's a list of notable conservative antigay activists who turned out to be gay themselves:

George Rekers:	Author of *Growing Up Straight,* contracted with male prostitute
Eddie Long:	Pastor and televangelist, was sued by four young men who had sex with him
Troy King:	Alabama attorney general, was caught in homosexual act by his wife
Richard Curtis:	State representative (California) caught with male prostitute
Ted Haggard:	Pastor, used male prostitute and drugs
Glenn Murphy Jr.:	Head of Young Republicans, performed fellatio on fellow Young Republican while he was asleep
David Drier:	Congressman (California) had sex with male member of his staff
Bruce Barclay:	Republican county commissioner, Cumberland County, Pennsylvania, was star in porn movies
Jim West:	Mayor, Spokane, Washington, twenty-five-year history of homosexuality

---

Even with all this evidence, and all these revelations, there are those who would still stand with conservative politicians and renounce the gay community while accepting the hypocritical behavior of their conservative representatives and leaders.

Several states in 2012 passed a gay marriage referendum. Among them were Connecticut, Iowa, Maine, Maryland, Massachusetts, New Hampshire, New York, Vermont, Washington, D.C., and two Native American tribes. Rhode Island and California recognize same-sex marriages performed in other states.

DOMA (Defense of Marriage Act) was passed on September 21, 1996, and signed by Pres. Bill Clinton. In 2013, the Supreme Court ruled that DOMA was *not* constitutional.

But the hot LGBT topic of 2016 seems to be North Carolina's House Bill 2. HB2, as it is commonly referred to, is a Draconian, stupid, conservative measure that the sponsors thought would sail right through and no one would notice, at least no one who had the power to do anything about it. Governor McCrory takes the cake. He's got to be living in 1985 or maybe 1885. He thinks that everyone has turned off their brain and will buy anything he says. I didn't think an elected official could be so wrongheaded.

After signing the bill titled "An Act to Provide for Single-Sex Multiple Occupancy Bathroom and Changing Facilities in Schools and Public Agencies and to Create Statewide Consistency in Regulation of Employment and Public Accommodations," which requires transgender individuals to use the bathroom of their birth sex, North Carolina experienced a wrath of hits from the business and the entertainment community. It was only then that they walked back the portion of the bill that would prohibit *state employees* from filing suit for redress of the law. *What an idiotic thing to do.* Does this man think we're all idiots? Does someone have to sit him down and tell him that companies and entertainers didn't decide to boycott North Carolina because North Carolina state employees were not able to sue under the provisions of this law?

Well, thank goodness that he's not president or king of the world; this way, only North Carolinians have to contend with this man, and hopefully, that's gonna be just for a few more months. But the greatest ruse of this law was that we citizens were supposed to be oblivious to the egregious parts of the law that would take away municipalities' ability to change certain laws without the permission of the state. The bathroom piece was supposed to captivate our attention so that we wouldn't notice that cities and counties wouldn't be able to do anything to affect critical issues like voting or taxation without the approval of those conservative legislators on Jones Street in Raleigh.

In comes now an openly gay organization that calls themselves Log Cabin Republicans.

Notwithstanding their support for the Republican Party specifically, and conservatives in general, Log Cabin Republicans remains on the fringes of the conservative movement and is outright rejected by many right-wing Republicans. Yet the clear majority of the LGBTQ community wholeheartedly support the Democratic Party and the candidates who run under its banner.

Chapter IV

G⁴
GESTATION
(Abortion)
Pro-Choice
Family Planners

Don't Bring Back Unsafe Medical Practices

Abortion is legal in the United States of America. But you wouldn't know it if you listened to the antiabortion crowd. They would have us believe that *Roe v. Wade* was something still being discussed, not the law of the land.

Conservatives' Connection with Gestation

Conservatives' commitment to the first "G" (God) has inextricably tied them to any and all pro-life positions, but particularly, it has tied them to their antiabortion stance. The further we go to the right, the loonier their stances become. For instance, Far-Right conservatives believe that there should be no abortions. *Period.* Not only would they disallow abortions paid for with public funds, but they would also outlaw abortions performed by private physicians on citizens with the acquiescence of their family and clergy. Aborted pregnancies that were derived from incest or rape would also be denied.

All these denials are linked to conservatives' belief that God is against abortion because <u>ALL</u> life is sacred in the eyes of God and abortion is murder. Conversely, most of these God-fearing conservatives are avid capital punishment advocates and have rarely seen a war they dislike. The linking of their religious belief with their position on abortion and pushing to have the federal government require all citizens to abide by their religious beliefs should be a violation of the First Amendment to the U.S. Constitution and deemed unconstitutional.

And although most Americans think it's all right for women to decide to have a legal abortion, conservative operatives continue using abortion as a wedge issue because it's "red meat" for their base, and it solidifies their relationship with the evangelical right. It also helps with the fifth and sixth Gs (genealogy and gubment). Many conservatives believe that too much public money is being spent on people who are not economically productive, and they think that most of these folks who are not economically productive are people of color.

Roe v. Wade

Roe v. Wade is the historic Supreme Court decision overturning a Texas interpretation of abortion law and making abortion legal in the United States. The *Roe v. Wade* decision held that "a woman, with her doctor, could choose abortion in earlier months of pregnancy without legal restriction."

Abortion is high on the list of "no-no's" in conservative theorem. They are led to believe that the act of abortion is an act against God and the value of life. But for too many conservatives, that sacrosanct commitment to life does not extend to life between birth and death.

Case in point: "Too many conservatives that have brought into the antiabortion argument also side with death penalty advocates, but even worse, many are generally against governmental programs designed to alleviate pain and suffering from the poor and disadvantaged. When voters vote for candidates who have campaigned on cutting the safety net for poor and disadvantaged people, not only is it not godlike, but they're also voting for the slow and miserable death of these people. These versions of "antilife" are just as bad as the wanton taking of life with lethal injection as is exercised during capital punishment. So one might ask "How can you be against abortion but for the death penalty and for Draconian governmental measures that strip the poor's safety net?"

Yet conservatives march to the polls every election and vote against candidates and for candidates simply based on their position on the abortion question. These are called single-issue voters. They feel so strongly about a particular issue that they become oblivious to other issues, such as wars, jobs, wages, infrastructures, affordable housing, and education, all of which can have a deleterious impact on the bottom line in households all across America.

How Republicans Used the Abortion Question to Further Polarize America

Republican strategists were well aware that the religious right had become a mainstay of the conservative movement, and one of the pillars of the religious right movement was their antiabortion beliefs. So if the Republican Party was to co-opt the religious right, they must become pro-life as a party. The pro-life mantra of the Republican Party has become a litmus test. It's gonna be very difficult to win in a Republican primary race as a pro-choice candidate on the abortion issue. So there's *Roe v. Wade*, and then there's the Republican Party. You'll have to decide which side you're on if you want to run in a Republican primary race. If you're thinking that the answer should be simple because *Roe v. Wade* is the law, you'll just have to think again.

Republicans don't stop with white working-class voters when it comes to the subjects of gays and abortion. They've attempted to gain entry into the black community with these two issues. The gay issue has gained a little ground, but the abortion issue was *dead on arrival* in the black community. Conservatives are gonna have to get something new if they want to expand their tent. And from where I'm standing, the 2016 Republican primary race shrank the tent instead of expanding it. These guys have got some tough sledding ahead. But it's like my dear grandmother used to say, "A hard head makes a soft behind."

Conservatives have used the abortion issue sparingly in the 2016 presidential primary races. It's not playing as well as it did a couple of decades ago, but it's still a vote getter. Conservatives tuck this issue away, close to their vest, so they can pull it out whenever they feel the need to.

They know what works and what doesn't work well. They know where it works better than other places, and they know which candidates could get the best mileage out of it.

Conservative campaign operatives are aware of these conditions and play them well during election campaigns. With the help of CAD software and geographically identifiable demographics, campaigns are able to send issue-sensitive campaign persuasion information directly to voters identified through "focus groups, polls, surveys, and voting history." This is why voters must start thinking for themselves.

Chapter V

G⁵
Genealogy

Genealogy (race, gender, and ethnicity): The generally accepted definition of genealogy is *the study of families and the tracing of their lineages and history.* But for the treatment of the term in this book, we will define genealogy as being the subtle (and not so subtle) denigration of men, women, and their racial, ethnic, cultural, and anthropological backgrounds for political gain. <u>*This chapter has been considered by many to the bellwether chapter of the book.*</u>

RACE

In 1779, Johann Frederick Blumenbach divided the human species into five races and called them the following:

- The Caucasian race or white race
- The Mongolian or yellow race
- The Malayan or brown race
- The Ethiopian or black race
- The American or red race

Johann Friedrich Blumenbach's racial identifications occurred when America was in her third year of independence and her 160th year of slavery. His initial and primary variable for racial separation was cranial size. There have been suggestions over the years that Blumenbach's assignment of cranial superiority was influenced by the economic and military prowess of the various races in 1779.

Racism has become a scary word in the modern political lexicon. People run away from the word even before they understand its true meaning. And because of this, now seems a perfect time to reintroduce and redefine the word "racism." If we replace racism with monoculturalism, it would make for a better understanding of the results of the practice of racism.

Monoculturalism can be defined as "the practice of elevating one particular culture (generally one's own) to a position of exultation, resulting in the stratification and degradation of all others." "Generally one's own" is a key operant phrase in the previous sentence. It opens the door for the consideration that, unlike racism, monoculturalists can be of any race, background, and culture. It would make it possible, for example, for an African to embrace Western civilization and therefore Western culture from a monoculturalist's prospective without any consideration of race. If today, however, an African American embraced European American culture to the exclusion of his own, he may be called an Uncle Tom. Monoculturalists strongly suggest (if not require and demand) assimilation into their culture by all other cultures. The culture practiced by Europeans (because of their global military conquest) has transformed itself into the standard by which all other cultures are measured. Therefore, those practicing European culture are protecting Western civilization. So in effect, this whole thing called racism is really about the promulgation of Western civilization. There are people we label as racist who deny that label vehemently because they see themselves supporting what they consider to be a superior culture, not a superior race. And if they allow nonwhites to participate in their culture as equals, then they're not racist. But they seem to be unaware that the practice of Western monoculturalism requires the exaltation of the white race.

During Europe's period of exploration from the fifteenth to the nineteenth centuries, when she came across artifacts and ruins of other cultures that were superior to known European civilization findings, they attempted to destroy or misrepresent their findings to maintain their sense of European cultural superiority. And still today, we find European monoculturalists promoting their brand of politics, economics, language, legends, sports, entertainment, and religion and, above all, RACE, to the rest of the world at the cost of culturecide to all other unlike cultures.

The antidote to monoculturalism is obviously "multiculturalism." Those practicing monoculturalism must come to know that monoculturalism is a formula for constant disrespect, tension, conflict, and, ultimately, war. It would appear that "multiculturalism" is the only answer and key to peace.

The following is a fictional accounting of how right-wingers make the connection between race and the six Gs:

"**God** meant for the races to be separated. When law and order breaks down, we'll need our **guns** to fight off the marauding hoards that descend upon us from the inner cities. **Gays** don't seem to care about color or race; they're just as bad as Ni**ers. If we could keep the colored races from fornicating so much, they wouldn't need to murder babies by **abortion**. Speaking of **race**, I'm not sure if we didn't perform a great global humanitarian service by taking this land away from the reds and the browns and having the blacks and the yellows work it for us. The current state of the American **gubment** is to take care of the coloreds. We work hard and make the money, and the government just **gives** it to them."

Race has become the rallying point around which the different factions of the conservative movement coalesce. Race is the lynchpin that holds the conservative movement together, not just the fiscal conservatism they would have you believe. It's the invisible, unspoken litmus test used by the movement, and it's the singular point of focus that keeps the conservative movement on the same page at the same point in time. Racism is real for conservatives, and it's the one thing that they'll deny exist within their movement until their dying day.

How did racism get its foothold in the *New World*? Well, let's see. The word had spread about the *New World*, primarily in Europe, and many saw the settlement of the *New World* as an answer to Europe's warmongering problems. "If all white people could unite under the same banner, it might save thousands of lives." If we fast-forward to the seventeenth century, we find that the natives of the *New World* were considered to be "others." All persons of African descent we considered to be inferior and meant to be subservient to the superior white race. Persons of Asian descent were good at working on railroads, doing laundry, and otherwise serving the superior white race. These racial views became codified in American law and calcified in American culture. Although not specifically mentioned in the constitution, slavery was the fulcrum upon which the entire South rests. Article I, Section II, Clause 3 of the Constitution reads,

> *Representatives and direct Taxes shall be apportioned among the several States which may be included within this Union, according to their respective Numbers, which shall be determined by adding to the whole Number of free Persons, including those bound to Service for a Term of Years, and excluding Indians not taxed, three fifths of all other Persons. The actual Enumeration shall be made within three Years after the first Meeting of the Congress of the United States, and within every subsequent Term of ten Years, in such Manner as they shall by Law direct. The number of Representatives shall not exceed one for every thirty Thousand, but each State shall have at Least one Representative; and until such enumeration shall be made, the State of New Hampshire shall be entitled to choose three, Massachusetts eight, Rhode-Island and Providence Plantations one, Connecticut five, New-York six, New Jersey four, Pennsylvania eight, Delaware one, Maryland six, Virginia ten, North Carolina five, South Carolina five, and Georgia three.*

The framers of the Constitution were very careful *not* to mention the word "slavery."

But for those informed citizens who could read, and bothered to read the Constitution, it was no secret what "all other Persons" meant. But I think if there was one word that united whites against *others*, it would have been "fear." Whites were (rightfully) fearful of the natives; after all, they took their land. Whites were also fearful of those they enslaved (the Africans) because of the close proximity that whites and Africans lived. Africans cooked and served their meals, they delivered and tended their children, they watched over them in their sleep, and they help them during their infirmities. Each of these circumstances gave Africans opportunities to injure or kill their enslavers, and some took advantage of the opportunity.

Fear, and the resulting aggression that followed, became an integral part of American culture. If you were white and didn't embrace the notion of fear and aggression, you ran the risk of being asked "the" question "Who's side are you on"? So if you were white, you wanted to ensure that "the" question was never directed toward you. You therefore exhibited behavior that made it very clear who's side you were on by using words, such as "ni**er," "chink," "injun," and "half-bred," and treating all people of color as if they were subhuman.

It's difficult to pinpoint exactly where, when, and what precipitated the race issue as the fulcrum upon which everything else balanced for conservative politicians. Some say it was the Sovereignty Commission, some think it was the Civil War, and all that led up to it. There are even those who say it was the Southern Manifesto, but most agree that although it may have started with either of the aforementioned, it clearly reached its maturity with the Southern strategy.

The business of race, among conservatives, goes back to a time before the founding of this country; it goes back to that peculiar institution— slavery. The profiteers from slavery knew that slavery could only exist if Africans could be looked upon as less than human. They knew further that the institution would be challenged by slaves themselves unless they could be psychologically controlled. Both happened; whites became convinced that slaves were not human, and black were brainwashed to think of themselves as less than. Blacks saw their masters as superior beings, they came to the conclusion that escape was a futile notion, and they therefore resigned themselves to a life of utter misery and found salvation and freedom in the afterlife offered by the religion granted them by their masters—Christianity.

Many thought that a union victory would bring about freedom and justice for the African and his cause of equality. The official end of the Civil War brought about a cessation of battlefield brutality and wanton loss of life; it reunited the union, so the North was satisfied, and after Reconstruction, the antebellum social order was restored, so the old Confederacy won the cultural war. So it could be said that everybody won something except African Americans. In many cases, post-Reconstruction life was worse than the hopelessness of antebellum plantation life.

When slavery officially ended on December 6, 1865, with the ratification of the Thirteenth Amendment, most slave owners and racist whites who didn't own slaves were Democrats. They didn't switch their party allegiance until well into the turn of the next century. Most African Americans were Republicans obviously because of the protections granted them by the GOP under Abraham Lincoln. Pres. Franklin Delano Roosevelt's "New Deal" made African Americans take another look at the Democratic Party. Pres. Harry Truman's executive orders outlawing racial discrimination by federal contractors and the desegregation of the U.S. Armed Forces was a huge measure attributing to the switch of African Americans from the Republican Party to the Democratic Party. As African Americans began to flood the Democratic Party, conservative whites began to feel uncomfortable and ultimately left the party for the open arms of the GOP.

But the greatest switch of parties came with the establishment of the "Southern strategy." And although the Southern strategy was the brainchild of Harry S. Dent Sr., many others played significant roles in its ascendency (Lee Atwater, Karl Rove, Ken Melhman, and others), but none played a greater role than Kevin Phillips. After the 1965 Voting Rights Act was signed, Republicans wondered what they should do about the newly registered black voters in the South. Phillips's answer was simple: "The more Negroes that register as Democrats in the South, the sooner the Negrophobe whites will quit the Democrats and become Republicans. That's where the votes are. Without that prodding from the blacks, the whites will backslide into their old comfortable arrangement with the local Democrats." Kevin Phillips's words were prophetic. And beginning with the first presidential election after the signing of the 1965 Voting Rights Act *(the Humphrey-Nixon election)*, the Southern strategy became legend in American presidential politics.

Lee Atwater

As to the whole Southern strategy that Harry S. Dent Sr. and others put together in 1968, opposition to the Voting Rights Act would have been a central part of keeping the South. Now the new Southern strategy of Ronald Reagan doesn't have to do that. All you have to do to keep the South is for Reagan to run in place on the issues he's campaigned on since 1964, and that's fiscal conservatism, balancing the budget, cut taxes, you know, the whole cluster.

The Republican Party began exploiting the racial climate in the South in 1968. There were, of course, several cases and situations in which race was used to gain political advantage long before 1968, but in 1968, it became an official and central plank in the platform of a major campaign—the presidential election in 1968. Other elections with heavy racial overtones were 1876 (brought about the Tilden Hayes Compromise and the end of Reconstruction, 1896 (this was known as the white supremacy election), 1972 (this was the "law-and-order election"), 1980 ("the granddaddy of them all, this racial election hid behind faux fiscal issues that Reagan's primary opponent, George H. W. Bush, called voodoo economics), 1988 (this election was about the Willie Horton attack), 2000 (this was the national coming-out election of the grandmaster, Karl Rove. Rove used race in Florida to win the election), and 2004 (Bush used race in Ohio to win reelection).

Campaign Strategies

Nixon developed the "Southern strategy," which was designed to appeal to conservative white Southerners, who traditionally voted Democratic but were deeply angered by Johnson and Humphrey's support for the civil rights movement. Wallace, however, won over many of the voters Nixon targeted, effectively splitting the conservative vote. Indeed, Wallace deliberately targeted many states he had little chance of carrying himself in the hope that by splitting the conservative vote with Nixon, he would give those states to Humphrey and, by extension, boost his own chances of denying both opponents an Electoral College majority. The "Southern strategy" would prove more effective in subsequent elections and would become a staple of Republican presidential campaigns. Nixon's campaign was also carefully managed and controlled. He often held "town hall" type of meetings in cities he visited, where he answered questions from voters who had been screened in advance by his aides.

In another campaign promise, he pledged to end the draft. During the 1960s, Nixon had been impressed by a paper he had read by Prof. Martin Anderson of Columbia University; Anderson had argued in the paper for an end to the draft and the creation of an all-volunteer army. Nixon also saw ending the draft as an effective way to undermine the anti–Vietnam War movement since he believed affluent college-age youths would stop protesting the war once their own possibility of having to fight in it was gone.

Using race as a wedge issue in national politics didn't begin with the Southern strategy. It had its beginning in slavery itself, and even before slavery, it started with a group of Portuguese sailors who captured several Africans and returned them to Portugal to perform free labor; this was in 1441. And then there was the *Dred Scott* decision, *Plessey v. Ferguson*, Black Codes, Jim Crow, the White Citizens' Council, the Sovereignty Commission, and the Southern Manifesto. But a good starting point might be the three-fifths citizenship rule or three-fifths compromise. This rule gave Southern congressmen an unearned advantage in the House of Representatives. The old Confederate states consequently had more representative power than their Northern counterparts with similar white populations. The three-fifths rule allowed states to count slaves as three-fifths of a whole person (for census purposes) in determining the total number of representatives and Electoral College votes authorized by the various states. Southern states needed to keep the socioeconomic and political circumstances emanating from discrimination, oppression, suppression, and subjugation of persons of African descent static if they wanted to continue their culture and social practices. They were successful, some say too successful. Too many of the racial attitudes and practices that defined the nineteenth century are still with us today, two hundred years later, as we embark upon the twenty-first century. How long will we allow race to define who we are as a modern nation state who seeks to rebuild the world in its own image? Do we really want the rest of the world to practice racial discrimination as we do?

Gender

Where do we start? The Nineteenth Amendment, ERA, gay rights? Just where do we begin? The "Right" has to be very careful with their treatment of the gender question. They have to convince the electorate that they're not against women while at the same time embrace time worn and outdated standards that *always place the man in leadership positions.*

There are more women than there are men in the United States of America, but men rule the roost. There are more women than men, but men make more money for the same work. There are more women than men, but the door is closed to women on certain career paths and individual positions.

Conservatives hide behind the Bible on issues of equal pay and other measures of gender equality. Unfortunately, conservative women don't challenge their conservative brethren on this and other issues that affect their conservative sisters.

Females comprise 51 percent of the population in the United States of America, and yet they presently only makeup 10 percent of governors and 22 percent of lieutenant governors. We've had one female Speaker of the House, and there has never been a female vice president or president.

Republicans cannot win national elections without considerable support from women, and yet we find that GOP policies tend to be antifemale, and they get away with it. They get away with it because of the same reason that they get away with embracing policies that are economically devastating to white working-class voters and still manage to garner their votes—"distractions." In the case of women, they have another incentive for voting against their gender interest; it's called the husband. White working-class males exert considerable pressure on their spouses to vote to protect "their way of life." Republican men have become successful at convincing their wives and other females that the survival of the white race is somehow dependent on the election of conservative candidates to office.

Women garnered the vote with the ratification of the Nineteenth Amendment. Prior to 1923, women participated in political campaigns; they even ran for political offices that they couldn't vote for. When they did exercise their right to vote, they were closely monitored by their husbands and other males. In some instances, Republican and Democratic polling places were in different locations, making it easy to know who you voted for. But there was another position taken by conservatives that didn't and doesn't sit well with women, and that's the notion that women are somehow less than and should therefore take on different responsibilities than men. In the twenty-first century, this position is not tolerated by most women. Conservatives are finding it increasingly difficult to honor the culture of the old Confederacy while respecting the modern aspirations of the majority gender on issues of equality, fairness, and justice, not only for women but for men of color as well. This is proving to be a very special problem for conservatives.

Women have held the following national and state and local offices:

1. Secretary of state
2. Various cabinet offices

3. Speaker of the House of Representatives
4. Governor
5. Lieutenant governor
6. U.S. Supreme Court Justice
7. And many other offices but not president or vice president

ETHNICITY

The issue of ethnicity has drawn greater consideration recently with the immergence of Hispanics as the largest minority group in the United States. White Americans have a new worry. First, it was the Native Americans, and then Africans and Asians, and now it's the brown people to our South. Whites in Europe comprise about 7 percent of the world's population, while North America comprises another 5 percent. This, coupled with other whites in the world who've left Europe and relocated in other countries of color around the world, brings the white population on planet Earth to a grand total of about 15 percent. This, along with the fact that genetically speaking, whites have comparatively recessive genes. All this is not a good combination for world domination. And yet it seems that white supremacists think that it's possible that the 15 percent will rule the 85 percent indefinitely and forever. Thank goodness for sound-minded whites and honorable people of color who oppose this notion of white world dominance. These are the real protectors of the white race. The super conservatives, right-wingers, and other bigot-minded groups and individuals serve no purpose other than to give white people reasons to distrust and fear the majority humanoid population.

The best way to ensure the survival and protection of the Caucasian race on planet Earth is to reverse segregation and incorporate all races into the one *human race*. If white people on planet Earth plan to survive, they must *join* the human race and not seek to manage and control it.

Chapter VI

G6
Gubment

The use of the word "gubment" (a colloquial pronunciation of the word "government") is not intended to marginalize, impugn, or denigrate anyone, especially Southerners. It just happens to be the way some Southern politicians have pronounced the word, oftentimes in *disgust* and many times used as a pejorative. Furthermore, it's ironic that the majority of social programs managed by the government are directed toward and created for the benefit of the very people who've been deceived into thinking that these programs are harmful and unnecessary—*the white working class.*

Gov. Ronald Wilson Reagan ran his campaign for the presidency on the notion that "the government can't solve problems because government **is** the problem." This proclamation became the rallying cry for conservatives and took the government haters to another level. They hated everything that wasn't capitalistic or conservative. They didn't like Medicaid, Medicare, Social Security, the Department of Education, ATF&E controls, or the dreaded IRS. They seem to believe in a very strict form of capitalism that disallows any public intervention in the market place (laissez-faire run amuck). Yet they don't explain how they would operate the roads without some governmental intervention; or raise, feed, and equip an army; or inspect food and other consumable goods and services, not to mention how they would refrain from asking for TARP monies when the banks go bust again.

It seems that the only way to prove to the laissez-faire hard-liners that this system won't work is to let it go and render the economy and civilization (as we have come to know it) nonfunctional. But Democrats aren't willing to go down that road, so they keep trying to "change the tires on a moving vehicle." It's a tough job, but I guess somebody's gotta do it.

When Democrats controlled both houses of Congress and the presidency, Republicans had reason to hate government because they didn't control it. But after they came into their own in the executive branch and took back the house in 1994 and the Senate in 1998, they had no need to hate government because they *were* the government. But they managed to switch gears again and let the Gs do their bidding for them. They represented government but managed to deceive voters into believing that government was not them but something that Democrats and people of color wanted and managed and that the GOP was here to protect them from the government. This approach begs the question "Is it at all possible to enlighten those who would fall prey to the hogwash spewed out by the conservative movement?" This may best be answered with a statement by George Will, the conservative columnist, former Republican, former Fox News commentator, and current MSNBC contributor. Will stated, in response to a question regarding reasoning with supporters of Donald Trump, "You can't use logic to dissuade individuals from positions they've arrived at through illogical means." A historically great literary mind spoke on this subject as well: "It's far easier to fool someone than it is to convince them that they've been fooled." This quote was by the great Mark Twain.

Government programs, including all entitlement programs, are mainly consumed by white people, and yet conservatives have convinced large numbers of low-information white working-class people that it's those lazy people of color who are using all the benefits that white tax dollars are used to purchase. But the truth of the matter is something totally different. The majority of adult Americans (55 percent) have received some sort of governmental benefits.

Of the fifty-one million Americans living in abject poverty, thirty-five million are white. So how is it that conservatives are able to easily convince (election after election) poor whites of North Carolina, South Carolina, Georgia, Florida, Alabama, Mississippi, Louisiana, Texas, Arkansas, Tennessee, Missouri, Kentucky, and West Virginia to vote against governmental programs used to help the poor? And why do they vote against candidates who want to help the poor? Again, the answer is "distractions." And although the answer is very clear, the Democrats' strategic response is very murky. Democrats would like nothing better than to convince working-class whites that people of color aren't their enemy but poverty is. But since the mid-1960s, Democrats have seemingly been afraid to attack Republicans for their antipoor stances. Maybe it's because Republicans always accuse Democrats of playing the race card when in fact, Republicans have made a political living off the race card. Without this card in their arsenal, they could not have attained the political heights they've attained over the past one-hundred-plus years.

Without governmental programs, the United States of America would be a country of a different color, and I don't mean racially. The chart below shows each state's population, the number of people in each state receiving benefits from the Supplemental Nutritional Assistance Program (SNAP), and the percentage of the total state population receiving SNAP benefits. What is also interesting is the voting records of each state and whether they supported the presidential candidate who wanted to reduce or eliminate SNAP benefits.

The states that historically vote for the Republican candidate are the very states that have the largest percentage of their people receiving SNAP benefits. The old Confederate states are among the highest. The chart of "SNAP Benefits by State" listed in Table 1a indicates that those state with very high SNAP participation rates voted for the party that vowed to reduce or eliminate SNAP.

STATE	SNAP %	PRESIDENTIAL CANDIDATE VOTED FOR IN 2012
Mississippi	*22*	*Republican (G1, G3, G5)*
Tennessee	*20*	*Republican (G1, G2, G5)*
Louisiana	*19*	*Republican (G2, G3, G4)*

Alabama	*19*	*Republican (G1, G2, G3, G5)*
Florida	*18*	*Democrat*
South Carolina	*17*	*Republican (G1, G2, G5)*
Arkansas	*17*	*Republican (G2, G3, G5)*
North Carolina	*16*	*Republican (G1, G2, G4, G5)*
Texas	*14*	*Republican (G1, G2, G3, G4, G5, G6)*
Virginia	*11*	*Democrat*

The analysis above is an example of people voting for the Gs and against their economic self-interest. The numbered Gs indicate which Gs were used incessantly by Republicans in political campaigns in that state.

Additionally, the U.S. Census Bureau, State and Local Government Finance report released in January of 2015, clearly establishes that the states that rely the most on federal aid are the states of the *ol' Confederacy* and other states that have traditionally voted with conservative Republicans since 1965. The figures listed below indicate the percentage of each state's budget that is derived from federal aid contributions:

Mississippi	45.3%
Louisiana	44.0%
Tennessee	41.0%
South Dakota	40.8%
Missouri	39.4%
Montana	39.0%
Georgia	37.9%
New Mexico	38.6%
Alabama	36.5%
Arizona	36.5%

There were 9 of the top 10 *(New Mexico being the exception)* recipients of federal aid that have overwhelmingly voted for the Republican candidate in each presidential race since 1968. These are the same people who claim that Democrats are the tax-and-spend crowd, and their taxes are going to lazy people in the inner cities. Well, it seems that it's just not true. It appears that the cash transfer is actually going the other way. It's the Democratic white, black, brown, yellow, and red people in all the other states that are transferring their hard-earned dollars to the conservative states of the ol' Confederacy.

There's a table published by the Pew Research Study that indicates that SNAP (food stamps) recipients are spread far and wide and that the greatest correlation is the Southern states appear to be more dependent on SNAP provisions than their Northern neighbors. And yet politicians campaign on planks that deride food stamps and pledge to cut them off if elected. But the biggest, craziest thing about all this is that the very people who are receiving the subsidies are the ones voting to elect the congressman who pledges to take away their food. Go figure.

Another study debunks the notion that people receiving benefits are lazy, don't want to work, and sit around, waiting on a handout check. Clearly, two-thirds (62 percent) of recipients are disabled, beyond working age, or are presently working and yet qualify for Supplemental Nutrition Assistance.

Republican strategists must know that they have a "good thing." They convince white working-class voters who're either receiving governmental benefits or have relatives or friends who are to vote for them. While they're voting for these scoundrels, these politicians promise that if elected, they'll slash or completely remove the same federal aid that's keeping their families alive. They end up voting for conservative candidates who run on a platform that sounds like this: "Vote for me and I'll lower your taxes. America's taxes are too high because of tax-and-spend Democrats. Democrats tax hardworking middle-class Americans (which Mr. White Working Class is not a part of) and then waste it by giving it out in gubment programs to the undeserving unemployed freeloaders, which Mr. White Working Class **is** a part of).

Just how long do conservatives think they can continue hoodwinking their base? Well, it's been going on for some time now, and it'll probably continue for the near future. But if their base ever wakes up, it's "Katie bar the door" for the Grand Old Party. And that time could be in November of 2020.

But the elephant in the room when we're discussing government and government spending is the DOD (Department of Defense). The United States of America spends more money on its military than all other countries of the world combined. The current U.S. budget has decreased from the Reagan era high of seven hundred billion to now just under six hundred billion. But we're still outspending all others, and we still call it the *Defense* Department. We have military personnel and/or DOD facilities in over seven hundred locations around the planet. And we tell one another, "This is for our *defense*."

The United States of America is the world's lone superpower, and therefore, our *real* purpose and goal is to stay on top. We're not out to stop country X or Y from invading us. And there's no real threat of country Z overthrowing our government. The practicable purpose for all these troops and facilities is to maintain the status quo indefinitely, which is impossible. The only "constant" in this universe is "change."

America's defense budget dwarfs all others, and yet it is treated as a sacred cow when it comes to meaningful and needed budget cuts. Bloated DOD budgets are a result of aggressive lobbying by defense contractors. Defense contracts have been awarded to companies to provide armaments and weapon systems that the generals don't want and have stated that these weapons are not needed. So do the politicians have greater knowledge than the generals about the needs of the military? Who are the politicians getting their military updates from? Who is advising them that more and different weapons are needed? Could it possibly be the former generals or the lobbyists who work for the defense contractors?

Many attribute the Iraq war to Cheney's ties to Halliburton. Vice Pres. Richard Bruce Cheney, the forty-sixth vice president of the United States of America, almost single-handedly started the Iraqi war. With little and, in most cases, no evidence that Iraq possessed weapons of mass destruction, Cheney pushed, cajoled, and coerced the intelligence communities to find information that would corroborate his assertion that Iraq had and was planning to use weapons of mass destruction against its neighbors and against the United States of America. As we now know, all this was a complete and totally fabricated *lie*. But that didn't stop millions of lives from being lost, billions of dollars lost and wasted, and the loss of international credibility.

Conservatives took a beating in the Vietnam War, but they learned a great deal that they put to good use in the Gulf Wars. First and foremost, they learned how to control the media. Conservatives credited the media with turning the American people against the prosecution of the war in Vietnam. During the Vietnam War, the media had considerably more freedom than did the media covering the Gulf War. Gulf War correspondents were embedded with preselected military units that had the effect predetermining news reports that Americans saw on their evening news. The Pentagon therefore control what was seen, and more importantly, they controlled what was not seen. This was the beginning of a new conservative effort to manage the media instead of having the media manage them. This is what Vice Pres. Spiro Agnew was trying to do and what Donald Trump seems to be doing very well. One of the best examples of the media being had took place in March of 2017. The media was getting hot on the trails of a connection between the Trump presidential campaign and the Russian government. Donald Trump decided that they were getting too close, so he tweeted at 3:00 a.m., "I was illegally wire tapped by President Obama during my presidential election campaign." This unsubstantiated, nonsensical allegation was picked up by *ALL* news services, completely knocking the Russian collusion story off the front pages and creating a frenzy among media outlets to research the possibility of President Obama creating a crime by illegally wiretapping candidate Trump. This would make a fantastic novel if it weren't so critically serious.

Afterword

Donald Trump has become the forty-fifth president of the United States of America. <u>NOW WHAT,</u> for the GOP, for Democrats, for the country, and for the planet?

American Polity was built on the two major parties forgoing differences after an election and getting back together to manage the country for the benefit of all. But it has become increasing difficult to coalesce after an election. Mitch McConnell (majority leader of the United States Senate) pledged on day 1 of the Barack Obama administration, "To, at all cost, make Pres. Barack Obama a one-term president." We've become so polarized in our political positions that the losing side would seem to be committing political heresy to work with the incoming administration. If it gets any worse, it'll be like a nation of monks teaming up with a victorious Nazi group to help them accomplish their goals, which would be close to, if not totally, impossible.

I cohosted an election night political "countdown to victory" talk show on WFXC-WFXK, Foxy 107.1 FM and 104.3 FM to celebrate what we thought was going to be the election of America's first female president. But things don't always work out as planned, especially in the political arena. Instead of electing the nation's first female president, voters elected one who is arguably the least qualified person to ever become president-elect of the United States of America.

Mr. Donald J. Trump was elected president, elect by a margin of 74 Electoral College votes (306–232). But he lost the popular vote by almost 3 million votes (65,844,954-62,979,879). Trump won Pennsylvania's 20 Electoral College votes by approximately 44,000 votes, Wisconsin's 10 Electoral College votes by approximately 22,000 votes, and Michigan's 16 Electoral College votes by approximately 11,000 votes. So a shift of 77,000 votes would have given Hillary Clinton an additional 46 Electoral College votes, bringing her total to 278 Electoral College votes, which is 8 more than would have been needed to become the president-elect of the United States.

Demographics are available to suggest how and why Mr. Trump won the Electoral College. One thing we do know is that pollsters and pundits had it all wrong. As of November 7, the day before the election, the polling firm "270 to Win" compiled the averages of 6–10 polls in each of the battleground states. The results are striking. The day before the election, "270 to Win" had Clinton and Trump tied in Florida and in North Carolina. They had Clinton up by 4 in Pennsylvania, up by 6 in Michigan, and up by 7 in Wisconsin. And as we all now know, the Secretaries of State in all five states reported that Trump had emerged the victor. How strange!

But be that as it may, Donald J. Trump was sworn in as the forty-fifth president of the United States of American at noon on January 20, 2017. And somehow "this too shall pass." And in the meantime, we must be extra vigilant in our pursuit of freedom, equality, and justice. We must shed the attire of Neville Chamberlain and adorn the cloak of Rosa Parks and Martin Luther King Jr. Now is no time to quit, compromise, or give in; it's time to take a stand for what we believe in, even if taking a stand means injury, imprisonment, or even death. "For what worth is life if everything you do and think, and everything you are has to be done within defined terms and conditions that require the approval of others." As the late Malcolm X so eloquently phrased it, "Unless you're a man that stands for something, you'll fall for anything." Everybody that lives dies. So the real question is not how long we live but "How did we live, and for what did we live?" Living for one's family and friends and all those who are oppressed as we are connotes a life of value without the fear of death. It is the fear of death that makes men become weak and allows others to control them through threats as though they have the power to immediately end our lives or allow us the opportunity to live in splendor eternally. We seem to forget that we all will die, even those who threaten us with death must someday themselves die. Lose your fear of death, and you'll gain real freedom. In gaining freedom, you'll acquire real equality, and equality brings on the justice we all are due.

The Republican Right (since 1964) has wagered the entire farm on the hope that the masses will never awaken from their slumber of stupor. They gambled that white working-class Americans will never figure out that the Gs have been, and are being, used to win their votes and keep conservatives in power. And through it all, the conservative ruling class within the Republican Party doesn't aspire to the same principles that they're selling. They're not overly religious, and they may or may not own guns. Many are homosexual or have family members and close friends who are. Many of them have had fetuses aborted, and the only thing that most of them seem to agree on is their latent *white supremacy views* and disrespect for people of color (this includes *conservative* people of color) and, most importantly, their laissez-faire attitudes regarding the role of government in the lives of citizens.

Now that we can see the *real* strategy of the Republican Right, it may become clearer to some that the elephant in the room (pun intended) has always been race, white privilege, and white supremacy. The election of 2016 bought it front and center (least ways by use of the "dog whistle"). While Democrats were focused on Trump's inexperience, his gaffes, and faux pas, the media was trying to get him to apologize for **SOMETHING, ANYTHING**. Instead, he's double down. "The Donald" and his surrogates introduced some new terminology. There's no such thing as *lies* anymore; what replaces lies in Trump's etymology of American polity is something called alternative facts.

The media maintained their vigilance; after all, Donald Trump was a rating's magnet unto himself, and they couldn't seem to resist the windfall of wealth he generated for them through the mega ratings they received while covering Mr. Trump. So when he tweeted his "dog whistle" messages to the soft racists (racists who don't commit acts of racial violence, so they don't consider themselves racists regardless of the bigotry, hatred, discrimination, and inequality they foster) among us, the media saw it as news so they carried his message (unedited) throughout the known universe, *at no cost to him*. The media gave Mr. Trump more free media than they gave all other presidential candidates combined.

Getting back to race, the Trump campaign knew from the beginning that if they could get enough soft racists to the polls, they could win, hands down. Democrats didn't believe it was possible because they put their faith in the "polls." The polls, as we have learned, were just a little bit off, by about 180 degrees. Poll designs are driven by assumptions. If assumptions are made, that hardcore racist won't show up at the polls in great numbers, and that soft racist will split along known ethnic, gender, age, and geographic lines, and then Trump's "dog whistles" and David Duke's enthusiasm would not affect the race.

Democrats also fell for the distraction that white working-class voters were supporting Trump because he was gonna bring back jobs. They knew he had about the same chance of bringing back jobs as Barack Obama did or, for that matter, as much chance as Hillary Clinton would have had. What these voters who talked about jobs really wanted was protections for their *whiteness*. They could accept being poor, being underemployed, even being jobless, but what they couldn't accept was being any of the aforementioned without being recognized for their God-given badge of whiteness. S while Democrats were scurrying about, trying to come up with an economic plan that included a considerable increase in the number of manufacturing jobs that didn't require a college degree, Donald Trump and his alt-right gang were feeding racial red meat to the same demographic. To the Democrats' surprise, the underemployed white guy seemed to have been more interested in his whiteness than in his pocketbook. Score up another misread for the Democrats!

Conservatives have also gambled that the common man will never figure out the complex economic system under which he lives. The predatory capitalistic system practiced by the United States is slowly but surely becoming a global system. And how many octogenarians would have ever thought that they'd live to see the day when Moscow and Beijing would have *day trading markets*? Yes, predatory capitalism has grown to rein supreme. But what now? Everyone knows that predatory capitalism is not good for workers, but they continue to support it with their votes and their very lives. Philip Kotler, in his book, <u>*Confronting Capitalism*</u>, discusses, in great detail, how race and ethnicity actually trumps dollars and cents.

So many may blame Republicans and other conservatives for the distractions used to gain political and economic power, but there's another entity that should not go unmentioned. That entity is what some called the fourth branch of national government, "the media." The media was almost solely responsible for the political ascendency of Donald Trump. Without the media's cooperation and lust for ratings and the money that those greater ratings would produce, Mr. Trump may not have even been an also-ran.

Right after the March 15 "Super Tuesday" primary race, a media report showed that Mr. Trump had received more *free media* than all the other presidential candidates combined. What did this mean? First of all, Trump was a media entity himself, having hosted several television shows, game shows, and been in the real estate market for years. This was too much for the media to turn down. All they could see was *"great big dollar signs."* Furthermore, they weren't about to lose market share to their competing media concerns. So they had to get involved with the new game in town, the Donald Trump sweepstakes. But this was politics, and the media should have another role to play in politics. That role should be to help the very people who help them get rich—the viewers, readers, and listeners. The help that people need is a complete and thorough vetting of all candidates. This vetting helps voters decide for whom to cast their vote. Unfortunately, that wasn't to be in 2016. Donald Trump ran roughshod over the media. He insulted, dismissed, embarrassed, and otherwise disrespected media personalities as though they were nothing. I've seen what can happen to celebrities who take on the media, and it ain't pretty. The one that comes to mind readily is baseball player Barry Bonds. Bonds's attempted fight with certain media personnel ended up (for now), leaving Bonds out of the Hall of Fame. But in the case of Donald Trump, there was absolutely nothing he could say that was so hideous that the various media outlets would figuratively castigate him. He felt he was invincible. He said after one of his primary victories, "I believe I could shoot someone in the middle of Fifth Avenue and not lose any votes." And you know what, he may have been right, but did the media cease upon this and make it an issue? Not on your life. They still allowed "the Donald" to do and say whatever he chose to do and say and get away with it. The media's greatest sin was allowing Donald Trump set the tone and choose the subject matter of the day. In media, we have a slogan we use to designate whether a particular subject or issue is worthy of continued coverage. We call it "having legs." In the case of Donald Trump, he decided when the media could leave a particular subject or issue and what the replacement would be. Sometimes I wonder if specific reporters were assigned to Donald Trump's AM Twitter monitoring brigade. They seemed to have been *starstruck* on each and every utterance.

This may be the first time someone has run for the presidency of the United States of America and literally told the media, the party he was running in, and the general public to "'Scuse me, 'scuse me, go take a flying flip," and not suffer any repercussions for it. But let's not rush blindly to blame Donald Trump for where we are and where we're headed as a nation. Donald Trump came just twenty thousand votes short of amassing sixty-three million votes. Donald Trump, presumably, only cast one of these votes, which means that there are lots of people in America who subscribe to the idiotic rhetoric spewed out by Donald Trump and Steve Bannon. And we need to fix this problem before we stitch up the patient and send him home with hands full of pain killers. In other words, this problem won't be fixed by going to the polls and electing someone other than Donald Trump. Those sixty-three million voters didn't actually vote for Donald Trump; they thought they were voting to save their culture and their race. Donald Trump could have been replaced by Timothy McVeigh, Terry Nichols, Dylan Roof, or Jeffery Dahmer. So our challenge is to enact policy to prevent the likes of the aforementioned from becoming elected to very high office. This is what the Electoral College should really be used for.

The media should have been vetting Donald Trump and all other candidates on their economic plan, their foreign policy agenda, and their plan to improve our crumbling infrastructure, improving K–12 education, making college affordable for all, paying livable wages to women as well as men, and reforming our criminal justice system. But instead, American voters were treated with every bombastic, idiotic tirade that Trump could utter. The media should be ashamed of itself for allowing Donald Trump to get away with the statements (and lack of statements) he's gotten away with.

The media has made hundreds of millions of dollars from advertisers because of the increased ratings brought on by covering Donald Trump, but has the media done its job of keeping the public informed and standing for truth and honesty? I don't think so. They've made lots of money, but they've made it at the expense of those whom they are supposed to be serving. They've treated the 2016 Republican primary and the general election as though it were some sort of "reality show." And for this, they should really be ashamed!

The Future of the Democratic and Republican Parties

Obama 332, Romney 206! That was the final tally of Electoral College votes for the 2012 presidential election. This wasn't exactly a landslide, but it was a prime-time thumping, especially when so many right-wing pollsters and talking heads predicted a Romney landslide. And even two weeks after the election, there were prominent Republicans who were still making excuses for Romney's defeat, everything but "He lost."

Republicans going forward have to deal with a demographic problem. Just about all demographers agree that somewhere around 2045, whites will cease to be the majority racial group in America. Hispanics' and African Americans' rise in population, coupled with the reduction of whites, will mean that for the first time in the country's history, whites will not have the numerical advantage to determine the outcome of elections on their own. The electoral implication is that Republicans (who depend heavily on the white vote) will have to venture outside their base to win elections. *This is a good place to interject the fact that the GOP's dependency on the white vote is one of the causes of tension between the races in America. It is politically beneficial to the Republican Party if the races see each other as the problem. Republican have won countless political races by stoking the fires of racial mistrust.*

Republicans will have to learn to court the "voter of color" (black and brown Americans). This is gonna be tricky in that the current conservative base is not in bed with Hispanics or African Americans. Republicans' entire approach to distracting low-information working-class whites with "dog whistle, sound bites, and bumper sticker slogans" will have to change. And in their attempt to expand their tent to welcome voters of color, will they lose more white voters than they gain in new voters of color? It's tricky. But this is where Republicans find themselves today. It reminds me of the old basketball adage: "You live by the jumper; you die by the jumper."

To understand the actions, motives, and strategies of Democrats, you need to first look at situations and circumstances through Republican lenses. And before we do that, we should take a quick scan of recent political interparty history. It could be said that many Democrats think that the purpose of government is to create and maintain circumstances that promote a climate of fairness with special emphasis on providing for those who've been historically disadvantaged (either by happenstance or by conscience deliberation). Democrats have, since the passage of the 1965 Voting Rights Act, aggressively gone after the black vote. The 1968 general election was the first election that showcased the potential power of the black vote. The black vote influenced politics in state and local elections as well as on the national level. Many Southern states witnessed the election of African Americans to state legislatures, boards of country commissions, city councils, and even to the position of mayor of major cities. But the GOP decided *not* to compete with the Democrats for the black vote; instead, they decided to use the marriage of blacks and Democrats as a wedge issue to pry away "Blue Dog Democrats⁴⁷" from the Democratic party, especially in the old Confederate states. This was the first step in solidifying the **solid South**. In the 1968 presidential election, Richard Nixon used coded language to engage the soft racist of his day. "Law and order" was code for "I'm gonna arrest, lock up, and otherwise stop the lawlessness coming from the black community in the inner cities before it spills over into the communities of our good citizens." This referred to the inner-city riots following the assassination of Dr. Martin Luther King Jr. "Entitlements" was code for "I'm gonna stop all the free services (welfare, food stamps, medical services, and other services used by the poor) that go to undeserving lazy folk who refuse to work." (Of course, the unspoken inference was that black people were lazy, didn't want to work, and received undeserving assistance that they thought they were ENTITLED to.) And the media failed to do its job to point out that the vast, overwhelming majority of entitlement recipients were white people. "Silent majority" was code for "Although your view isn't being carried by the media, and you're not out in the streets protesting and rioting, you're still the majority in the country, and the majority still rules. We need to bring back white rule. We need to make America great again!"

Just as Donald Trump refused to show his taxes in 2016, and bragged about his secret plan to destroy ISIS and bring back manufacturing job to America, in 1968, Richard Nixon had a secret plan to end the war in Vietnam. When Nixon's reelection came around in 1972, he hadn't ended the war in Vietnam, the economy was ruinous, and crime was higher. So how did he get reelected in 1972? Nixon used "DISTRACTIONS" as well. The year 1972 marked the beginning of the ascendency of the National Rifle Association, and Nixon (although raised as a Quaker) appeared to have been joined at the hip with Evangelicals Billy Graham

---

47 "Blue Dog Democrats" are democrats that are devoted to their party (won't change party affiliation) but consistently vote for the more conservative candidate—usually the Republican candidate.

and Jerry Falwell. He also never let an opportunity go by to deride black people or black culture while extoling the virtues of Western culture and Western civilization. And of course, to soothe the hunger pains of the plutocrats, he offered tax relief to those who didn't need it, at the expense of those who would be hurt the most by tax cuts for the rich. So it's clear that distractions are not new conservative strategies but have been deployed for decades before Donald Trump. We all should therefore expect a continuation of *distractions* under a Trump administration.

This approach may explain why women, minorities, and the poor generally flock to the Democratic Party. And if this depiction is accurate, what would be the motivation for people to seek membership in, and protection of, the Republican Party? Let's first look at the well to do. Many financially well-off people in America are attracted to the GOP because they believe if the Democrats have their way, they'll lose in the zero-sum game of wealth redistribution. So no matter how we slice it, it's still all about *MONEY*. There are millions of people who seem to feel that without interventions from the government, they will always do very well. They therefore abhor any and all government intervention, except deregulations, building infrastructures, taxing the masses, enforcement of favorable international laws, and huge tax cuts for the wealthy.

But things weren't always this clear-cut. The GOP was the brainchild of Francis Preston Blair. With the implosion of the Whig Party, Preston Blair started the Republican Party in his living room in 1854. The essence of the party was conservatism and holding antislavery positions. One of its leaders and party spokespersons was Abraham Lincoln. But things have changed dramatically since 1854. Many of the original Republicans would today be Democrats, and just about all Democrats in the later part of the nineteenth century would be Republicans today. When the die-hard fiscal and social conservatives left the Democratic Party for the new Republican Party in the latter half of the twentieth century, they took everything with them except the name. The final nail in the plank that changed party affiliations in America was the 1965 Voting Rights Act. Richard Nixon was well aware of the change presented by the 1965 Voting Rights Act, right on the heels of the 1964 Civil Rights Act, and how it would be accepted around the country in general but particularly in the South. It became very clear (from that point forward) which side one should be on, and race played a very large part in this decision-making. So here we are today, more than fifty years after the demarcation lines have been set, still playing the party games with the labels of race, wealth, and status.

Democrats have been aware of, and participating in, this interparty political game for some time now; they just have not been able to come up with a strategy to win consistently. If the GOP's prime directive is to stop redistribution of wealth, the Democrats appear to have settled on a strategy of acquiring and maintaining a numerical majority. They also seem to want to attract new party members by appealing to their sense of fairness, justice, equality, and democracy. Republicans know they can't win the numbers game (there are substantially more disadvantaged people than there are people who are well-off), so they have to change the rules of play, how the game is played, and why. The first thing Republicans want to do is reduce the number of voters, and if given a choice, they'd much rather reduce voters in the areas that generally vote democratic (voter suppression). The next step is to determine for whom votes are cast (packing), require specific measures that have a higher likelihood of affecting Democratic voters than Republican voters (voter's ID), and the list goes on and on. But if all this fails, Republicans still have their ace in the hole, "distractions." Republicans have become experts at distracting low-information voters by use of social and moral issues.

The sixth G, gubment, can be classified as a distraction that falls under the fiscal realm, and the other five Gs are social and moral. The second and fifth Gs, guns and genealogy, are both social issues, while the first, third, and fourth—God, gays, and gestation (abortion)—are moral issues. So how does the GOP appeal to voters who should be voting against them? They appeal to them by using social and moral issues. They use the first five Gs to distract them from the sixth G. This strategy seems to work because many voters are *single-issue voters*. They become so embroiled in one of the social or moral issues that they literally don't care what the GOP does about all the rest as long as they're with them on their single issue. Republicans have done an excellent job with these people, and Democrats don't seem to have any answer other than registering more people and getting them to the polls to vote, especially people of color. This plays right into the hands of the GOP when it comes to their social campaign; they just plug in the fifth G, genealogy, and the low-information white voters eat it up.

Many political observers thought that the Sandy Hook Elementary School shooting would have been the event that turned the NRA on its head and took the guns distraction from conservatives. The reason it didn't happen was because there were too many single-issue voters who had brought in to the notion that big government was going to take their guns away, leaving them vulnerable to attacks from the criminal elements of society. So we tolerated the shooting of five- and six-year-old children so that voters wouldn't be worried about criminals being the only ones with guns.

What should the Democrats' response be to the NRA thumbing their noses at them? Maybe they should first stop taking campaign contributions from the NRA. And if they refuse to walk away from the NRA trough, then maybe they *should be* <u>*primaried.*</u> Being primaried is a tactic almost exclusively used by the GOP. Democratic officeholders seem to instinctively know that there's no penalty or price to pay for being elected by Democrats and then acting as if you're too afraid of Republicans to carry out your constituents' wishes. What about growing a little backbone?

Why do Democrats seem to spend all their time trying to find common ground with the Far Right? The Far Right knows the game; they know that all they have to do is *wait and obstruct, and obstruct and wait.* Republicans know that the Democrats' prime directive is to get them (Republicans) to become bipartisan and get things done through compromise. They know that Democrats want bipartisanship so badly that they're willing to cave in on just about every single program or promise they've made to their constituents. Republicans know that Democrats have never seen a compromise they didn't like. They know that Democrats value compromise above everything else. Republicans therefore use this fact to manage the Democrats and get what they want, even when Democrats control the majority in both congressional houses and the White House.

Democrats are going to have to come up with a strategy to get things done without caving in to the right. Tom DeLay said, "We should not measure our representatives by what they're willing to compromise or give up but by the conservative values they refuse to relinquish to our detractors." I don't agree with Mr. DeLay on most issues, but this is one I'm willing to reconsider.

Democrats are going to have to reconsider their approach to compromise and bipartisanship. The leadership in the Democratic Party must realize that Republicans are not staying up all night, trying to figure out ways to compromise with Democrats or create new opportunities for bipartisanship. Once Democrats realize and accept this as fact, then and only then can they embark upon the trail of advancing the platform of their constituents. Democrats appear to be tied at the hip with the ideas of bipartisanship and compromise. They tend to think that these two principles are the essence of democracy, and without them, the system won't work, and that might be true, but your opponents have access to your playbook, and they've devised a plan to block, inhibit, stall, and otherwise kill any and all Democratic plans and programs. They've understood that if Democrats' main causes for existence is compromise and bipartisanship, all Republicans have to do to thwart those plans is say no. Democrats must realize that *unilateral compromise* is tantamount to capitulation, and *unilateral bipartisanship* is an oxymoron.

What has happened in the past is this: Republicans hear that Democrats are about to introduce a bill or measure, and they need Republican support. Republicans stake out a position far right of the Democrats' position and wait for the Democrats to do their thing, compromise. This strategy results in a "center-right" final solution. Democrats seem to have an internal battle before they present their measure to the Republicans. When those who want a liberal or far-left position make their proposal, they are counterweighted by those who say that "the Republicans will never go for a liberal, far-left position, so let's water things down and move closer to the center." So Democrats present a centrist proposal, while Republicans continue to hold out for their far-right solution. The middle ground between these two positions is "center right." This is not good for the Democratic Party leadership, but more importantly, it's awful for the Democrats' constituency. It makes things appear that it's always a win-win situation for Republicans, and a lose-lose situation for Democrats, no matter who's in power.

Democrats seem to be unable to understand that some of their constituency think they're keen on compromise and bipartisanship, to a fault, the fault of *capitulation*. Democrats need to understand that bipartisanship and compromise are *means and methods*; they should not be destinations and goals unto themselves. Democrats need more leaders who want to be judged by what that are *unwilling to compromise on* instead of leaders who seemingly want to see how much they can compromise for the sole sake of bipartisanship.

Students of the American political system are well aware that without compromise, the American two-party system is incapable of producing a governing government to solve the nation's problems. Conservatives are also *well aware* of this and use it to get Democrats to bend to their will. Threatening to shut down the federal government is a good example of just how far conservatives are willing to go to win. Conservatives want to win by any means necessary. They therefore force the American economy to the brink and wait for the Democrats to cave, for the sake of the country. What if the Democrats don't cave? What if Republicans don't budge? Do you think that Republicans are willing to see the whole country go under if they don't get their way? Well, that's what they want the other side to think. It's sort of like this grand plan of political chicken or splitting the baby and giving half to each claimant. Republicans, by their actions, believe that Democrats will always cave to save the baby.

After the Democrats lost five of six presidential elections from 1968 to 1988, they must have decided that the country had gone to the right, and they themselves must move more to the center if they wanted to win. In came William Jefferson Clinton and the DLC (Democratic Leadership Council). But things actually began in 1984 when Pres. Ronald Wilson Reagan ran for reelection. Reagan was coming off a resounding victory over incumbent president Jimmy Carter. Democrats knew they needed a strong comeback, or the electoral momentum would swing decidedly to the Right. But they were "capped"[48] by election protocol, which meant that the leading candidate to beat was the vice president on the most recent presidential ticket. That individual was Walter "Fritz" Mondale of Minnesota. The 1984 election turned out to be worse than the 1980 landslide. In 1980, Reagan garnered 489 Electoral College votes, while Carter managed only 49 Electoral College votes as an incumbent. But in 1984, Reagan collected **525** Electoral College votes to Mondale's poultry 13 Electoral College votes. After President Reagan handed Mondale his head, Democrats decided they needed to make some changes. They decided that they needed to move closer to the center. They came up with a group that labeled itself "the Democratic Leadership Council" (DLC). Some of the prominent members were Al From, author of *The New Democrats and the Return to Power*, Governor Chuck Robb of Virginia, Gov. Bruce Babbitt of Arizona, U.S. Senator Lawton Chiles

---

48 "Capped" is a term used heavily in African American and urban communities to denote prevention or obstruction.

of Florida, U.S. Senator Sam Nunn of Georgia, and U.S. Representative Dick Gephardt of Missouri.

The DLC recruited Arkansas governor William Jefferson Clinton to run for president in 1992. They felt that Bill Clinton was a perfect fit. He was a Southerner, he was white, and he had been elected governor of the state of Arkansas. And just as important was the fact that he articulated his message in a rhyme and rhythm that resonated well with the African American base of the Democratic Party. Clinton chose Sen. Al Gore of Tennessee to be his running mate. Neither of these two were flaming liberals, and that's why the DLC was delighted with them. They were the answer to the question of who do we choose to guide the Democratic ship back toward the middle. To some of the Democratic Party's base, Clinton appeared to be willing to do *anything* to keep the GOP from enveloping his right flank. This meant throwing Lani Guinier under the bus, outing Sister Souljah, and going toe-to-toe with Jesse Jackson. While in office, Clinton shored up his right wing by coming down on the conservative side of several critical bills and positions: welfare to work, the death penalty, and his signature on the Gramm-Leach-Bliley Act, which had the effect of repealing the Glass-Steagall Act. Glass-Steagall provided protection against banks and other financial institutions making risky investments with the deposits of citizen investors and governmental investors. Many economists fault the repeal of Glass-Steagall for the Great Recession of 2008.

Fast-forward to 2016: The DLC and plenty of politicos and pundits have rationalized that Donald Trump's political ascent is the result of his enormous popularity among white working-class voters. No doubt Trump is well liked by many college-educated Republicans as well, and his strength among those without a college degree is undeniable. But Trump ascended to the presidency because a very large number of Americans felt that they were losing their culture, especially that portion associated with race and ethnicity.

Hispanics weren't just taking jobs. As a matter of fact, most people who complained about Hispanics taking jobs wouldn't be caught dead in one of those jobs held by Hispanics. These people saw Hispanics using the money they made from those backbreaking jobs that nobody else wanted, to buy businesses, homes, and otherwise making themselves become a permanent part of Americana—language and all. Many whites saw African Americans rise to positions that they had never held before. They saw immigrants from Southeast Asia owning "Mom & Pop" operations, and they saw all this through the prism of a "zero-sum game.[49]"

I guess here is as good a place as any to discuss my greatest surprise of the 2016 presidential election, that is, 53 percent of all white women voted for Donald Trump. This is more than unbelievable for me; it's one of those things that I'll never get over. This demographic statistic goes to the core of my political belief system. I would have lost tons of money had I been asked to bet on the percentage of white women who would vote for Donald Trump. I still don't believe that 53 percent of all white women voted for Donald Trump after his misogynistic tirades with supporting video, and more than a dozen women who came forward and accused him of sexual harassment and sexual assault, that the majority of white women would go to the polls and cast their vote for this man to be president of the United States of America is UNBELIEVABLE! What do these women tell their daughters and grandchildren about why they voted for this man? The only thing I could come up with to remotely justify their decision is culturism and racism. I guess a sizable number of white women voted for their culture and their race instead of their gender or their party or, for that matter, their country.

In recent years, the correlation between party ID and educational attainment has grown. Essentially, the education gap has morphed into an education gulf. White women with advanced degrees are now one of the most faithful Democratic subgroups. According to data from the Pew Research Center, 62 percent are Democratic or lean Democratic. In the 2012 election, there was a thirty-point margin between how whites with a postgraduate degree voted compared to how whites with no college degree voted. But a GOP voter today is more likely to be white and working-class than a Democratic voter, and they still hold more political power than hypereducated white voters. So the candidate who can connect with them has an edge in the GOP primary, but it's a tall mountain to climb in the general election. If all this would have held true, Donald Trump would have won the Republican nomination for president but would have lost badly in the general election to Hillary Clinton. This didn't happen either. So how and why did Donald Trump win the 2016 general election for president of the United States of America? Let's take the why first.

---

49 "Zero-sum game" refers to the notion that for every winner or gainer, there must be a loser. Those who believe in this notion think that minority gains are taken directly from "hardworking white people."

Let's first admit that there are too many racist and bigots in America. No one knows exactly how many there are, but there are too many, and they're becoming more powerful. They're diminishing in total numbers, but they've added an element to their overall prowess that increases the potency of their dwindling numbers. They have become increasingly more wealthy. They've also managed to build a coalition with the wealthy.

This is what many African Americans heard from a collective white voice after the presidential election results were announced Tuesday night, November 8, 2016. Everyone, including the pollsters, were totally convinced that Hillary Clinton would be the forty-fifth president and the first woman president of the United States of America. It didn't happen. White America said, "We're gonna show you how it feels to have someone you totally abhor to become the president of the country." We could have had Jeb Bush, Ted Cruz, Marco Rubio, or even Mitt Romney, but we chose Donald Trump, not because we thought he was better than the rest but because we knew how much he would infuriate all of **YOU**. We didn't really think he could win, but the stars seemed to have lined up just right that night, and we got our wish. And now you have "the Donald" for the next four years or more. Some would read this and ask how could sane people who cared anything (not just about their country but) about the world risk all humanity to payback their detractors for electing an "N-word" as president, twice. And then there are others who know the vitriol of the haters; they know the loathing, unforgiving attitudes they bring with them wherever they go, and they expect nothing less.

On December 19, 2016, when the Electoral College vote was cast in the various states, Donald Trump received 304 Electoral College votes, while Hillary Clinton garnered 227. This act officially gave Trump the title of "president elect," which meant that he was scheduled to be sworn in on January 20, 2017. There were at least three other elections that had the racial impact as this election did. Obviously, the first Lincoln election of 1860 was instrumental in deciding the racial direction of the nation, and so was the election of 1864. But some would argue that the election of 1876 and its aftermath was just as traumatic, if not more so, than the elections of 1860, 1864. But I believe that history will show that all three elections pale in comparison with the "sea changing" election of 2016. Other elections that had obvious racial overtones were 1898, 1928, 1932–1948, 1968, 1972, 1980, 1984, 1988, 2000, 2004, and obviously, 2008 and 2012. The white supremacy election of 1898 saw the last African American elected to congress for just under three decades. It was also the cause of the *coup d'état* in Wilmington, North Carolina, in 1898 where white conservatives couldn't wait until March to have the newly elected official take office, so they threw out the defeated officeholders prematurely and took not only their political offices but also their personal properties (homes, businesses, and land). The general election of 1928 saw the election of the first African American to hold office in the United States Congress in almost thirty years. Oscar DePriest was elected to represent Illinois's first congressional district in November of 1928 and took office in January of 1929. George H. White, elected to the U.S. Congress in 1898 to represent North Carolina's Second Congressional District, declined to run for reelection in 1900, leaving the congress without any black representation until 1929. From 1932 through 1948, the New Deal ushered in the CCC, CWA, FHA, FSA, PWA, SSA, TVA, WPA, and HOLC and NIRA. Many would say that the SSA (Social Security Act) was the most effective and had the greatest positive impact on the recovery from the Great Depression. In 1968, Richard Nixon unveiled the *Southern strategy* and its racial overtones. In 1972, Nixon again reverted to race to win the election; this time, he stressed the "dog whistle" of *law and order and drugs, which meant arrest every black male you* can and keep him locked up for as long as you can. In 1980, Ronald Reagan became the "States' Rights" presidential candidate. He overtly sought the white racist vote, and he got it in 1980 and again in 1984. In 1988, George H. W. Bush used the image of Willie Horton (a black felon who allegedly attacked a white woman), and in 2000 George W. Bush won the presidency by using voter shenanigans in Florida's black community; and during his 2004 election, he won with the help of Ohio's Secretary of State, Mr. Kenneth Blackwell. Trump won in 2016 using race and racism as it's never been used in a presidential race before. Heaven help us! I'm not at all sure that the nation and the world will survive Donald Trump as president of the United States of America.

The End

Bibliographic Essays

Chris Hedges tackled the issue in his book *American Fascists: the Christian Right and the War on America (Free Press 2006)*. There was no trouble finding materials for the first "G" (GOD) in this book. The religious right has been working conservatives since the mid-sixties (c. 1965). He speaks eloquently about the war on truth. In reading Hedges, I came to realize that "cherry-picking" the Bible is not telling the whole truth. And furthermore, telling half-truths about any religion will eventually prove to be counterproductive.

Kevin Phillips is mentioned in several sections of this book because of the advisory role he played with the Republican Party immediately after the passage of the 1965 Voting Rights Act. But Phillips was also instrumental in crafting the Republican political position vis-à-vis the position of the religious community. In his book *American Theocracy: the Peril and Politics of Radical Religion, Oil, and Borrowed Money in the 21st Century (Viking 2006)*, he carefully outlines how Republicans might profit politically from a tighter alliance between the two.

At the confluence of God, race, and politics, Mark A. Noll inserts his predispositions in such a profound manner that it clarifies the individual meanings of the three while simultaneously merging the three in a seamless tapestry, which explains racial politics across the nation but particularly in the South. He was absolutely "spot on" by giving his book the title *God and Race in American Politics (Princeton University*

Press 2008). Noll makes a historical analogy between God, race, and politics and the various eras that they played out. Slavery, colonization, independence, Civil War, freedom, civil rights movement, and modernity are all discussed through the prism of God, race, and politics. And no doubt, the election of the nation's first African American president would have been discussed as well had the election happened in 2007 instead of 2008.

The New Jim Crow authored by Michelle Alexander and published by The New Press is a well-written classic on the subject of race and class in twenty-first-century America. Michelle holds no punches. She's extraordinarily blunt, precise, and on point. Her opening chapter titled "The Rebirth of Caste," lays the foundation for jaw dropping candor and eye-opening realism to an issue too long ignored and misrepresented. Professor Alexander carefully weaves and then brilliantly presents the seamless connections among *race and class, drugs, a race-based criminal justice system (which includes mandatory minimums), incarceration, prisons for profit, racial profiling, and police brutality and released from the system but branded for life.* This book is must reading for all concerned with race, class, and justice in the United States of America.

Thomas B. Edsall, in his book *Building Red America: the New Conservative Coalition and the Drive for Permanent Power*, analyzes the National Rifle Association's ratings of congressmen's and congresswomen's voting record on issues related to gun control. He correctly assigns a controlling position to the NRA vis-à-vis the Congress of the United States of America. His implication that the NRA is setting itself up as the unofficial fourth branch of federal government is striking.

Tom Hamburger and Peter Wallsten have collaborated on (what was thought of by George Will and others) to be the primer and roadmap for a new polity in America, one in which Republicans dominate and completely control. The title of their book is *One Party Country: the Republican Plan for Dominance in the 21st Century (Wiley Publications 2006)*. Hamburger and Wallsten highlight Karl Rove's address to the Conservative Political Action Conference in 2005 when he warns, "Republicans have now won 7 of the last 10 presidential elections. We hold 55 Senate seats, 232 House seats, and 28 governorships. These facts underscore how much progress we have enjoyed in the last four decades, and it has been a remarkable rise for our party and our movement. But it is also a cautionary tale of what happens to a dominant party when its thinking becomes ossified, when its energy begins to drain, when an entitlement mentality takes over, and when political power becomes an end in itself rather than a means to achieve the greater good." I ask if the Republican Party reached that point in the 2016 primary and general elections.

Nolan McCarty, Keith T. Poole, and Howard Rosenthal argue with the best tools of discourse—statistics. They show unequivocally that American has become more politically polarized over the past few decades. They begin with their baseline year of 1972, and over the proceeding decades, they show how much the country has become polarized. And they identify source of this ultra-polarization—the media and the conservative wing of the Republican Party. The media polarizes for excitement and drama, which increases ratings, which means greater profits. The conservative wing of the Republican Party creates polarization for survival purposes. Conservatives are well aware of the statistics that suggest that c.2045 whites will no longer comprise the majority of the country's population. Others (Hispanics, African Americans, Asians, and other nonwhites will collectively become the numerical majority. Conservatives have therefore concocted a plan to retain power even after they've become the minority. It's through "polarization and divide and conquer." The title of their book is *Polarized America: the Dance of Ideology and Unequal Riches (Massachusetts Institute of Technology, 2006)*.

E. J. Dionne Jr.'s *Why the Right Went Wrong: Conservatism—From Goldwater to the Tea Party and Beyond* is a good place to start when we discuss the craziness surrounding the 2016 Republican race for the presidency. E. J. has written many compelling books, essays, and articles but none as contemporary and relevant as this. This book was published by Simon and Shuster in 2016. In this book, he doesn't spare the roughness of the ride—from Goldwater to the Donald. He doesn't sugarcoat the hypocrisies, from Nixon to "W", and he is not afraid to cite the obvious—that the right is taking all of us down the wrong path.

Godfrey Hodgson is the author of one of my favorite book. The title, *More Equal Than Others*, says more than the entirety of many books. This book was published by Princeton University Press in 2004. Godfrey reminds us all that "The misdiagnosis of a problem is the same as refusing to admit that the problem exists." The truth of the matter is that America's original cry for freedom, justice, and equality was concerning the colonies and the British. White America in no-way intended to have freedom, justice, or equality for red, brown, yellow, or black people, just among the ruling class of Homo sapiens (Caucasians). After the general population in the colonies were convinced that they were not only equal to the British but were, in fact, far superior to the people of color that populated this new land that has been bequeath to them by God, it became difficult and next to impossible to reverse that course and ask the general population to accept the red, brown, yellow, and yes, black people as their equal. When, in fact, the superiority of whites over blacks was the cornerstone in the justification of the institution of slavery, which was the economic lifeline for whites in America. Fast-forward to 2016 and see how we're still struggling with the notion of all being equal, even after the election and reelection of our first African American president.

Daria Roithmayr has penned a well-researched book titled *Reproducing **RACISM**: How Everyday Choices Lock-In White Advantage*, published in 2014 by New York University Press. A quick listing of her chapter titles should give all who inquire an insight into her predispositions and concerns: I. The More Things Change, the More They Stay the Same. II. Cheating at the Starting Line. III. Racial Cartels in Action. IV. Oh Dad, Poor Dad. V. It's How You Play the Game. VI. Not What You Know, but Who, but Who You Know. VII. Please Won't You Be My Neighbor? VIII. **LOCKED-IN**. IX. Reframing Race. X. Unlocking Locked-In.

Reducing Gun Violence in America is a well-written book that not only covers the recent gun violence between unarmed Americans and the law enforcement community, but it also captures, quantitatively, the historical aspects of gun violence in America. Webster and Vernick use crosstabs to compare and contrast selected variables throughout the demographic diaspora. Their editing style is well organized, and they leave us with hope. The hope is that "with the courage to elect courageous leaders and representatives, American voters may get what they need, effective gun-control laws."

Neil Irvin Painter's *The History of White People* is riveting. She makes Blumenthal's *Races of Man* appear elementary. Painter explores the notion of race from its biological, cultural, geographical, and political origins. She exposes numerous myths about the origins of the concept of race differences and any predetermined biological stratification of the races. So many myths are exposed in Painter's treatment of this crucial subject that her book qualifies as a must read in all matters of race, culture and politics.

Slavery, Capitalism, and Politics in the Antebellum Republic, Volumes I & II by John Ashworth was a critical source document in the research of the cause and movements that lead to secession and war. This beginning was crucial because it gave greater understanding to the attitudes of postbellum Southerners during and after Reconstruction. Attitudes formed during and immediately following Reconstruction were the forerunners of Black Codes, Jim Crow, Segregation, and the all-encompassing racism still prevalent in American society today. Ashworth chronicles and documents how each element (slavery, capitalism, and politics) played individual and collective roles in the building of race relations as we know them now.

Edward H. Bonekemper III is a brilliant author who sometimes finds himself swimming upstream against the tide and in troubled waters. He finds himself in these conditions because he dares to take a contradictory position against the CV (Confederate Veterans), UCV (United Confederate Veterans), and the UDC (United Daughters of the Confederacy). These three organizations did more to determine how the Civil War and the Confederacy is remembered than any other organization on either side of the conflict. It seems that the union (USA) was satisfied that the Confederacy had surrendered and wasn't concerned about how many statues and organizations arose out of the defeat of a lost cause that intended to destroy the United States of America. Bonekemper takes umbrage with this approach and goes to great lengths to point-out and dispel notions of Confederate greatness and the righteousness of their cause. Bonekemper's book is titled *The Myth of the Lost Cause: Why the South Fought the Civil War and Why the North Won.*

Following up on the groundwork laid by Bonekemper, Edward Baptist laid out his treatment of the era in his description of the horrors of post-slavery enslavement. In his book *The Half Has Never Been Told: Slavery and the Making of American Capitalism*, Baptist makes the undeniable connection between slavery and American capitalism, both before and after the Civil War. Although Baptist's narrative is primarily anecdotal, the repetitive occurrences give added weight and dimension to the individual happenstances.

Off Center: The Republican Revolution & the Erosion of American Democracy by Jacob S. Hacker and Paul Pierson the "meat of the coconut" when it comes to describing conservative motives and plans to override Democracy and institute their political ideology despite their numerical shortcomings. Conservatives are by and large against civil rights, minority advancement, and egalitarianism. They therefore tend to attract those in the electorate with similar feelings and predilections. The South before and after the civil war became the nation's beacon for race-based politics. After the civil rights movement, it became more difficult to attract and maintain whites to a party that espoused racial discrimination and white supremacy. Conservatives began using diversionary tactics, tactics such as gerrymandering, voter suppression, and voter intimidation. And if that wasn't sufficient, they resorted to "distractions."

The Wrecking Crew: How Republicans Rule by Thomas Frank examines the exact method and plans used by Republicans to institute their social and economic ideology or see the country destroyed. Frank points to Grover Norquist as the architect of the plan to destroy liberalism in America by enacting "Tort Reform, Destroying Labor Unions, Strong support for NAFTA, School Vouchers, the elimination of the Departments of HUD and Education, and THE PRIVITIZATION OF SOCIAL SECURITY." They know that liberals will cave in right away when given the option of bending to conservative desires or seeing the nation drift into ruin. Republican uses this tactic unrelentingly to get their way without ever considering the effects of national disunion on the common man. It's almost like the biblical story of Solomon when he threatened to sever the baby and give half to each maternal claimant. In this case the true mother is the Democrats. Hope is still alive that Solomon (the American people) will notice the veracity and caring in the cry of the Democrats and render unto them the democratic union they love and cherish so dearly.

Endorsement

Val Atkinson's book cautions us to avoid losing focus on key issues that can both unite and move society forward. He provides a necessary history on how the ruling elite have often used wedge issues to divide the American public. Whereas many have written about the issues of "gays, gods, and guns" in recent elections as wedge issues, Atkinson expands upon this list. He provides context to these issues as a learning tool so that the reader can avoid succumbing to the will of the masters of distraction. In an age where the media is focused on 140-character messages coming from the White House, it would behoove the public/reader to pay attention to policies being considered in the U.S. Congress and in state legislatures and to remain focused on the pivotal issues, such as economic inequality, for example. Indeed, this is not to minimize the importance of social issues that are considered wedge issues; rather, it is to minimize efforts by the ruling class to use those issues to divide and to distract us. Val Atkinson's work provides key lessons from the past and a roadmap as we move forward into the future.

Artemesia Stanberry
Associate Professor of Political Science,
North Carolina Central University, Durham, North Carolina